RECIPE TO WIN THE UP ELECTION 2022

Demands of the Current Generation

PRAKHAR KISHORE

Notion Press

No.8, 3rd Cross Street
CIT Colony, Mylapore
Chennai, Tamil Nadu – 600004

First Published by Notion Press 2020
Copyright © Prakhar Kishore 2020
All Rights Reserved.

ISBN 978-1-64951-965-8

Dedication

To all the offices and departments, where I went and struggled to get my work done; to all the tables I had to go to which led me to understand the system, find ways to navigate it and helped me in writing this book.

Acknowledgements

I would like to thank my parents, my family and everyone around me who has taught me and supported me during the good and bad phases of my life.

Contents

Preface 9

About the Author 11

1. Introduction 13

2. Understanding UP 19

3. The Middle Class 31

4. The New Generation 33

5. The Solution 35

6. Government Management Service 37

7. The State Vision Fund 41

8. The State Vision Team 45

9. Business Development Department 53

10. Education 59

11. What Comes out Must Stay in 65

12. The Black Economy 67

13. What is Illegal, Should be Made Legal 69

14. The State Stock Exchange 73

15. The State Fund Management Team 79

16. The State Project Management Team 83

17. Government Switch 85

18. Policy Formation & Review Board 89

19. The Districts 91

20. Research & Development 113

21. Supercomputers & Data Servers 117

Glossary *119*

Preface

The essence of the book is to understand the poor situation of UP. We need to accept that and find a new solution to approach this situation. This is what the current generation needs to know what, how, when and where we need to improve on. This book is from my perspective and you may or may not agree with me. This book is just an illustration of what we can achieve. It is an intense operation towards bringing a reform that is necessary.

This book is dedicated to the common citizens. So, I have tried to use easy to understand words and have given examples where ever necessary. I have written this book to make people understand what the real problems are and how important it is that we resolve all the problems by finding the appropriate solutions to it. I felt the need that someone should address the issues in hand by writing about it and making people aware.

Why I think most economic laureates give inaccurate data is because their data is based on analytics which are given to them by the surveyors who have not put in much effort into their work to get the exact data, so it does not represent the majority and they are incapable of procuring new and accurate data as they don't know how to.

This book has no intention of endorsing or criticising any government department or organisation or any political party.

I have presented some solutions or ideas throughout my book. These initiatives can be taken into consideration to improve UP's situation to help overcome various obstacles. Economic growth is important because when there is economic growth, only then will we be able to develop our nation by exploring more avenues for jobs and revenue.

About the Author

Prakhar Kishore, Director at Hydrobull Group and a civil engineer has a keen interest in knowing things that are around and surrounds him. He observes and absorbs and he has an ambition for building his hotel, construction, capital investment, school and real estate businesses and work for the people. When he was 9 years old he read a story about Jamsetji Nusserwanji Tata as to how he founded the Tata group and made a business empire which made an impact on him. He wishes to travel the globe to experience things first hand. It is his first book and he has an inclination for writing about subjects that have moved and changed his perspective in life. He, as the name of the book suggests belongs to the state of Uttar Pradesh where he believe much efforts are still needed to be put in by the people and the government to help make it the golden state.

More into the practical life, life is full of lessons and these lessons keep us going. What builds up our personality is our practical journey and our day to day advents. Although emotions are invaluable, focusing on the practical aspect brings more clarity and gratification. He always has a very different outlook towards things going around him, very selective and precise about everything he does, he chose to be vocal about this very prime and ignored subject matter.

Growing up with a fascination towards new technologies and inventions, he is very much inspired by Mr. Ratan Tata. Apart from his business, he spends his time playing golf. If we were to describe him, words like generous, open hearted and friendly with people can be the best choice.

He also worked closely with the honorable **Member of Parliament Sri Ram Shakal ji**, towards the development of tourist circuit in Vindhaya Region which led to the formation of a project **Bhavy Vindhya Circuit** by his company which was much appreciated by him and the commissioner of Vindhyachal. Sri Ram Shakal ji understood the importance of project further raised a question in **Rajya Sabha on 06th August 2019** to seek this development in the region.

Always coming up with a powerful idea and finding the best solutions with a "never give up" attitude is his strength while being calm, opportunistic and positive is an icing on the cake.

Although his technical skills are better than his writing skills,

"Writing is not a profession but a state of mind to pen down beautifully," he says.

A thinker at mind, and practical at heart, his interests have always been intact in social causes, exploring more and grabbing knowledge about everything that concerns him.

Chapter 1

Introduction

The current situation of Uttar Pradesh (UP)

UP needs a person who can cure the problems of the state, someone who is able to understand what the weaknesses and strengths of UP are.

Let's take an example to understand the situation and think of it this way.

You go to a doctor and you tell him about a problem. He doesn't take you to the operation theatre and perform the operation right away, does he? He will first check for the symptoms that you have. He might use his stethoscope or other basic tools and instruments in hand to diagnose the problem.

Then if he is not able to figure out the problem, then he would recommend or perform certain tests. Using these test results, he would judge if it could be cured from medicines or if an operation is needed.

In the current scenario, the operation is performed first and then the result of its outcome is resolved.

Image source Census India

It is all done just to get instant results. But it is not something that should be executed in such a manner.

At times we see the problem but we are not able to resolve it due to the fact that we are not able to patiently diagnose and find a solution.

What we need to understand is that we all have our flaws.

- We will make mistakes.

- We can correct them.

- In some cases or situations, we may let them be for the time being.

Forgiveness is also a great power that we should use at times.

We are not super humans or gods. We are just humans we will make mistakes; we will learn, we will rectify; we will establish and conquer.

Aim

- Understanding UP.

- Looking at UP from a different perspective.

- Increasing the state revenue sources.

- Implementing new and improved policies.

- Establishing and exploring new opportunities and avenues for growth.

- Establishing new business sectors i.e. industries, offices, etc.

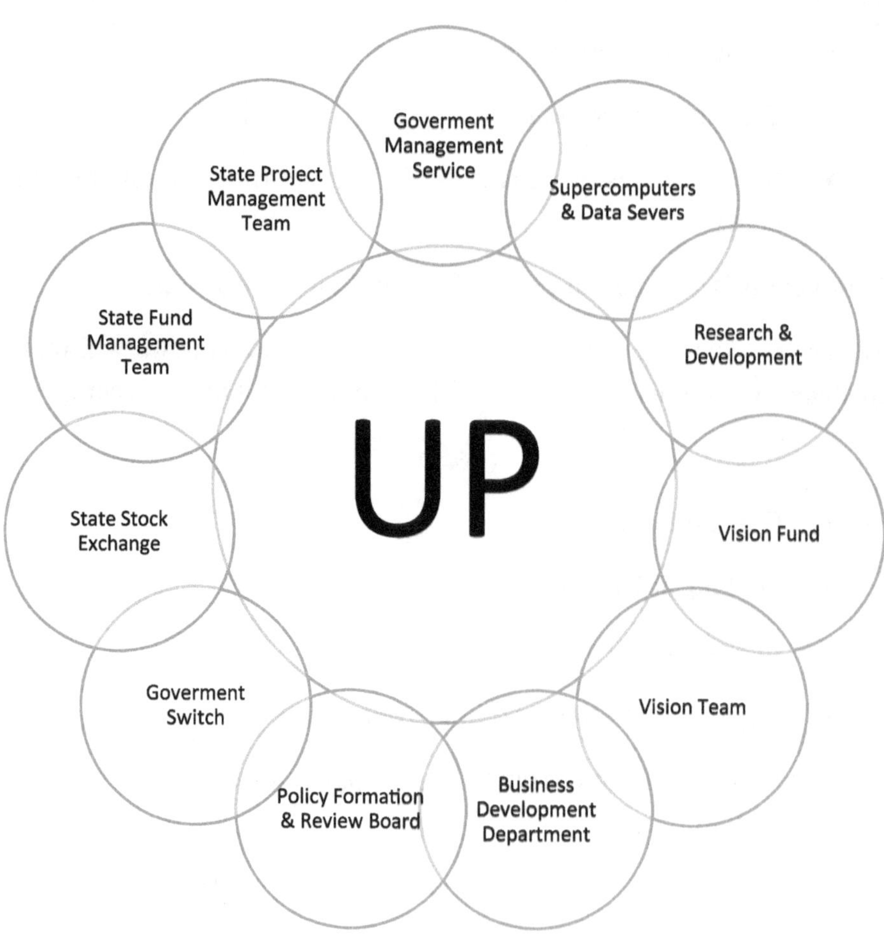
State Project
Management
Team

Goverment
Management
Service

Supercomputers
& Data Severs

State Fund
Management
Team

Research &
Development

UP

State Stock
Exchange

Vision Fund

Goverment
Switch

Vision Team

Policy Formation
& Review Board

Business
Development
Department

What is needed for a project to come into action?

Money: If there is no money in the state, there will be no growth.

How can a state make money?

The answer is simple. It is to help the business sector and they will, in return, help the state.

If you notice the proceedings of the state, you will notice a trend or a pattern that the money that comes in each year, for its development goes back to the source unused.

Why is that so?

What do we lack?

Can we improve the situation?

The answer to all these questions is:

Yes, we are lagging behind but we can definitely work our way to finding the appropriate solution.

"Jis Deshya Pradesh ki agar aarthik sthiti sahi hai,
toh uski maanasik sthiti bhi sahi ho jaegee."[1]

---

[1] If a country or state has less monetary issues, then even its citizens will have better peace of mind.

Chapter 2

Understanding UP

1st person: Aree saheb se aapki mulaakaat hai jara hamaare kaam ke vishay mein bhi baat kar leejiye ga aap. Aap jo bataenge vo kardenge bas bhagwan ki badee krpa ho jaayegi agar humaara kaam hogaya toh.[2]

2nd person: Aree aap bilkul bhi pareshaan maat hoye, aap bilkul sahi aadamee ke paas aaen hain aapka kaam toh hona hi hai aur ho jaayega. Bas jo aapko bataya hai usspe thoda dhyaan dijiyega. Baakee sari chinta aap hum par chhod dijiye.[3]

3rd person: Aree ye kya leke aaye ho mantriji ko chillar denge kya. Mantriji pichhali baar bahut naazaar ho rahe theh. Usse bolo ye humara thodee hai mantriji aur unake aadmiyon ke liye. Iss baar party fund mein humaare organisation se acha khaasa deposit maanga gaya hai. Ek kaam karo abhi ye rakh lo aur bol do bade saheb se baat karke approve karavana hoga agale hafte unake liye bhi kuch karna padega. File yahin table pe chhod do.[4]

---

2   Sir, could you have a word with your senior about my pending work? I will be really glad and happy that with the grace of god my work is done.

3   You don't need to worry about anything. Your work will definitely be done now that you have met me. I request you to fulfil the requirements that I mentioned. And you can leave the rest to me.

4   What have you brought with you? The last time mantri ji was very angry with it. You know this is not ours; this is for mantra ji and his people. This time the party

4th person: Iss bar itne hi budget se election kaise ladenge,pichhale saal ke fund mein aur iss saal ke fund mein bahut difference hai, isko cover karna padega aur kuch aur bhi badhaana padega nahi toh election haath se nikal jaayega. Banners aur hoarding sare district mein lagavaana hai kitne kharche hote hain tumhe toh pata hi hai. Ab batao kese hoga itne se mein?[5]

"Iss poore process meh kaam kahaan bola ek baar bhi"[6]

If we play a blame game, then whom shall we blame?

"Jo actually kaam karta hai woh sochata hai ki konasee aisee galatee hojaaye usase ki usakee naukaree chali jaaye."[7]

A few days back I wrote something to the Prime Minister which then came in the IGRS (Integrated Grievances Redress System). It was then forwarded to the concerned department. Let me share it here as well to just give you an idea:

Uttar Pradesh

Sir,

Considering the fact that the state of Uttar Pradesh needs to grow.

---

fund requires more amount from our organization. Do one thing, keep this amount and tell him that we will need to discuss with our seniors and only then will your work be completed. Leave this file on the table and go.

5   How are we going to manage this election with such a low budget? There is a huge difference in the amount we had last year and we have this year. We need to cover this gap and generate more if we are planning on winning this election. You already know how much cost we have to bear for the banners and other expenditure towards winning an election.

6   In this entire process, where did the work speak for itself?

7   The person who actually does the work will be wondering about what mistake he might end up making that will cost him his job.

Here are a few things I feel should be changed:

Uttar Pradesh, as we all know is famous for low cost labour. Gangsters and politicians combined control all the business sectors. Ease of starting a company is very tough. Even after so many efforts by you and your government and the people who try to put your thoughts to action, they are forced to be puppets in the hands of a few.

Age old policies are still in effect.

For example, consider the development authorities today are working on the plan, the structure and policies made a few decades back.

*Here is story: A woman of 30 wants to setup a ladies parlour in an area near her home. So she finds a good location for it. She rents the place, sets her shop and invests thirty five thousand rupees of her hard-earned money. She makes her company and sets her GST. After a few days into her business a letter comes in. It is from the development authority saying that her business is illegal and the place is not a commercial location. She is summoned on a certain date to the development authority court and is scared. She is standing in front of a judge who is not from a law background but is actually an engineer who scared about his job and has no capability of taking the right decision. When her name is called, "It has been only three days since I opened my shop."She begs and requests in front of everyone. He asks her to close it in the next three days. She leaves crying. Is this the ease of doing business? Now what happens after a few more court dates is that a babu from the office comes to her and asks her to come to the office the next day and that he will tell her a way in which she can still run her business. The next day with a strong bold heart, she meets the babu and he says **"Madam, dekhiye aapke kehne pe sir ko humne mana liya hai har maheene ka 5000 lagega aur kal se dookaan khol leejiye"**.[8]*

Construction in other developed countries is going way ahead but in our country it is way backward. The drawing we give to the authority needs

---

8   Madam, I have convinced my senior and he said that you will have to pay Rs. 5000 per month and you can open your shop from tomorrow.

approval. There is always a difference in the construction drawings and authority drawings because the authorities need their cut to approve them. That's the reason why these age old policies are still in place. Coming from a civil engineering background helps me understand this. Let any person construct anything if his foundations i.e. structural drawings are correct and considering the height of structure to foundation design ratios are correct. Construction technology has moved way ahead from the time this country is still in. These are the few factors why our structures are lagging behind.

In Lucknow and all the major cities in UP, there is a lack of industries. Why? That same woman's story applies to every department. Why does it happen? It's because the ministers need their part in the cake. Be it any political party, it's the same story for UP and hence no development happens. No one wishes to setup his or her industry here.

UP needs a TRUMP as its Chief Minister. Uttar Pradesh itself is a country. If you count its resources, it is endless. Beautiful places and plain fertile land. Low cost labour.

Listen to the middle class business man or business woman. Their story.

Add to that story, if that very woman could have easily setup her store, she would pay her taxes and hence increase revenue of the government and by the grace of god and your support, she opens up more shops from the profit and success of her shop and she would pay more and more taxes.

If you consider an example of a startup, they cannot afford a place in the starting, so where will they setup shops? Can they in their house?

Why I write to you, Sir Modi ji and Yogi ji is because I respect your vision and look to see our country to a great future. I have a few more ideas and would like to share with you via this channel.

Yours Faithfully

Prakhar Kishore.

The reply from that department is as follows:

प्रेषकः

सेवा में,
श्री प्रखर किशोर

नत्थीः...

विषय
आई0जी0आर0एस0 सन्दर्भ संख्या–600000200005016 द्वारा की गयी शिकायत के सम्बन्ध में।

महोदय,

कृपया उपर्युक्त विषयक स्वकीय पत्र दिनांक 10.01.2020 का संदर्भ ग्रहण करने का कष्ट करें। आप द्वारा आई0जी0आर0एस0 के माध्यम से यह शिकायत की गयी है कि एक महिला द्वारा आवासीय क्षेत्र में खोली गयी दुकान को ▇▇ विकास प्राधिकरण द्वारा भू–उपयोग के बावत एक नोटिस दी है। भारत में विशेषकर उत्तर प्रदेश में यह प्रक्रिया गलत है। सरकार ऐसी योजनाएं बनाये कि महिलाओं को बिजनेस सेटअप में आसानी हो।

उक्त के सम्बन्ध में अवगत कराना है कि महायोजना के अन्तर्गत भू–उपयोग निर्धारित किये गये है। निर्धारित भू–उपयोग के विरूद्ध यदि कोई आवंटी/व्यक्ति क्रियाऐं संचालित करता है तो नियमानुसार लागू नियमों एवं सुसंगत धाराओं के अन्तर्गत कार्यवाही किये जाने का प्राविधान है। तदनुसार कार्यवाही की जाती है।

अवगत होना चाहें।

भवदीय,

प्रतिलिपिः–अनुसचिव आई0जी0आर0एस0 को सन्दर्भ संख्या–90000200005016 निक्षेपित किये जाने हेतु प्रेषित।

In this letter, what the gentleman is trying to say is that if a person is running a business that is not as per the government rules and not written in by-laws, we will apply all the rules and acts to that person or her business and proceed accordingly. What we all know is that it is the standard procedure by the government. What I wanted to achieve with that letter is for the policies or acts and rules to be improved or changed for the betterment of our society.

> *"Yeh Niyam aur yeh Kanun humaare leeye hi toh banate hain, toh samay aur zarooraton ke hisab se inaka badalana bhi toh zarooree hai."*[9]

I don't blame the officer or the department because they don't have the time or the energy to reply to every comment or concern made by a citizen. It is very difficult to find a solution to all the problems at once.

> *"Bas apani kalam bach jaaye"*[10]

In present times major reforms and efforts have been put in by our government in various fields. It's not like change is not happening. It is happening and in the right direction too which is a good sign for growth. It was truly amazing to see that my letter reached the source which I was indirectly referring too. It's not the fault of the government if the particular department didn't have enough time to respond to the letter in the appropriate direction. So, I believe there is more room for significant changes to be made in certain areas. And I believe in our current leaders who are constantly working towards this direction. As we are constantly seeing drastic changes made by our leaders and taking such commendable decisions.

---

9 These rules and regulations are made for the public and should be changed when the public demands for it and changed from time to time with regularity.

10 Saving him from making a proper effort.

When and why do we need reform?

We are at a point where our country is stable and when things are working in a particular format but we see no sign of growth. And as a growing economy and a developing country, we can't be stable. There should be an urge for growth.

So, coming back to the point i.e. our state of UP and as we all know that we are a land locked state which means we are surrounded by land on all sides. The source for water is just the rivers.

Why are southern states of India more prosperous than UP?

They have oceans using which they are directly connected to other countries. So we see a greater amount of prosperity and growth in that part of our nation.

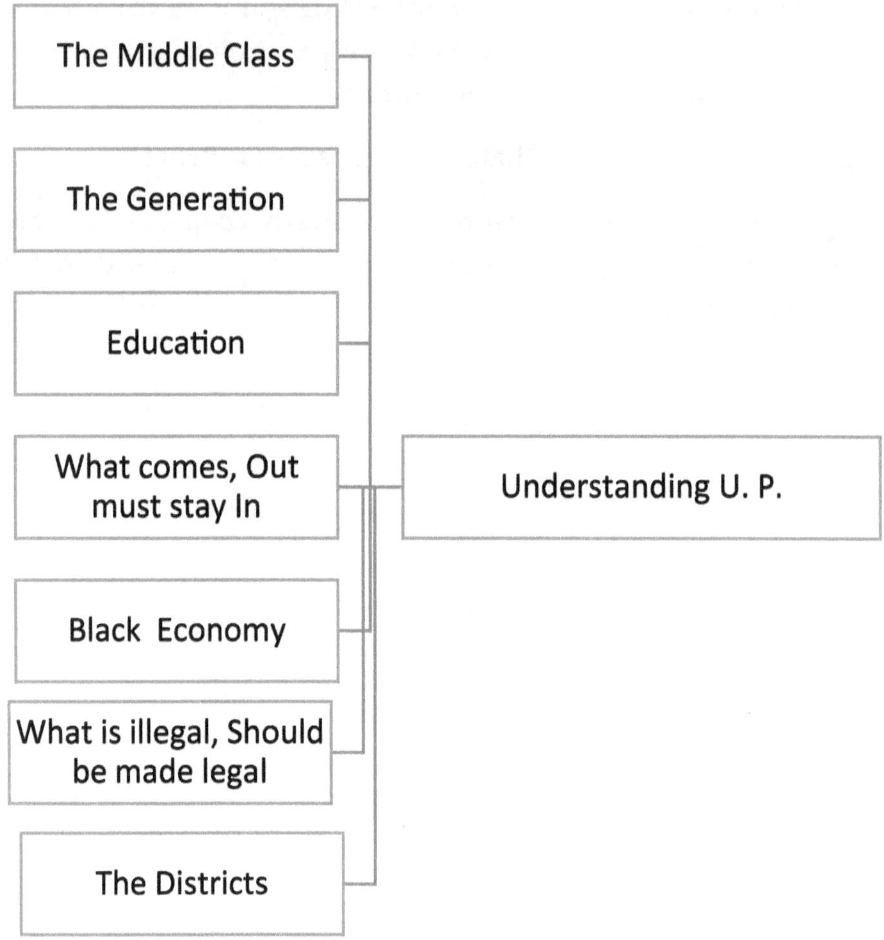

The Middle Class
The Generation
Education
What comes, Out must stay In
Black Economy
What is illegal, Should be made legal
The Districts
Understanding U. P.

What can UP Do?

1.   Manufacturing – Major source.

2.   IT Services or Backend services – Major source.

3.   Manufacturing of skilled youth. – Major source.

Adopt the generation and the generation will adopt you.

- Follow the trends.

- Working like a pro team.

Do we really believe and the country as a whole think that just the students of IITs and IIMs will bring the country, great success?

No, how can a student who has just one perspective in life which is studies, bring about change that is desperately needed. Do we really think bookish knowledge could bring about the change? That is completely impossible. We live in a country where bookish learning is given much more value than practical learning. New ventures in education are a necessity and a desperate need.

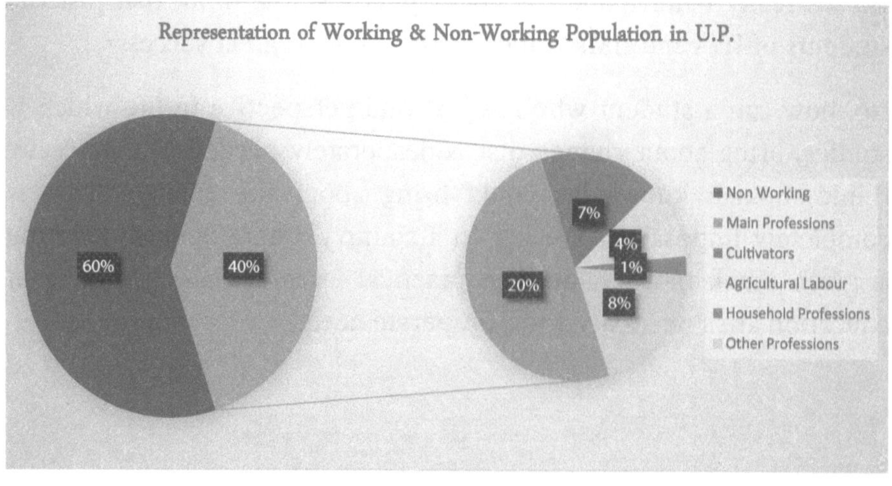

Based on Data available on Census of 2011

"Whatever you deliver today will reflect tomorrow."

What that means is that if you bring in numerous opportunities for the youth today, you will generate a massive return from the youth in the future.

Value education will change the perspective of the country. Value education is the same as the concept of value investment for better returns, if we just break things into little portions and let that individual portion grow.

For example: If you take 20 seeds, plant each of the seeds in different pots and add different compost to each one of them, then each seed will grow differently from rest 19. Now each seed has grown into a unique plant which is one of its kinds.

The requirement of fast investments and big investors in our country is a must.

Is it necessary?

Yes, for the growth of the state, the need for big investors is important because they bring new money into the state; the money which was not associated with that state earlier.

The need for organic investors:

The term organic investors define the people who are from the state who can invest. They have the capital and are ready to invest but due to lack of knowledge and support aren't able to.

"Janaab jo policy bana raha hai unakee toh har maheene ki tankha unake bank account mein credit kar di jaatee hai, unaka kya johar din chunautiyon bharee zindagi,roj chhotee chhotee cheejon ke liye jang lad rahe hain."[11]

Desh kon chalata hai? Who runs the country?

What will be your first thought? I guess that it would be politicians, bureaucrats and other powerful people, right?

Yes, they only control, but do not run the country.

But actually, peddle kon maarta hai?
(Bicycle)
It is the middle class.

How?

The middle class is directly connected to the lower class and the upper or the high class. This class which I am talking about is on the basis of income and not in terms of caste and creed. It is just generalisation of the class and further classification is unnecessary.

So, actual mein sunanee kisakee chahiye?[12]

The Middle class: The thought which the powerful people have, reflects on the upper class and the lower class through this class.

And we also need to update our state policies at every front constantly so that we keep up with the trends and needs.

---

11   The people who are making these policies are getting their salaries credited each month and are not affected by it. What about those people whose day to day work and lives are being affected and are struggling for the little things in life?

12   So actually who should the government listen to?

Chapter 3

The Middle Class

These are the people who work hard, pay their taxes and run the economy actually. They are actually the middle man between the rich and the poor. They can sustain anything, starting from harassments from the rich as well as the poor. They actually do most of the work, from listening to their bosses to managing their junior staff who resist doing their jobs.

"Yeh bechaare aise log hain jo agar 2000 rupiya lagake agar kaam hojaaye toh badee mushkil se aur seene pe patthar rakh ke de dete hain,ki hey bhagawan bas mera ye kaam karva dena"[13]

"Dard hota hai uss paise ka jo mehanat se kamae ho"[14]

Nobody wants to live in the same stature their entire life. Everyone needs and deserves a chance for jump or growth in their lives. No one wishes to work where there is no scope for success.

A lower class person wants a life of a middle class. A middle class person wants to live a life of an upper class person.

---

13 These people are so poor that if a work requires an amount like 2000 rupees, they give the amount with a very heavy heart and pray to God that the work gets done successfully.

14 We feel the pain in giving away the money which we earned with a lot of hard work.

The maximum number of people who pay taxes in our country is the middle class. It is because of their taxes that the country makes most of its revenue. So, listening to this class becomes crucial for the government and from their earnings, the lower class makes their earnings as well.

So, who is going to be their saviour or their superhero?

Is it going to be the government or the Netas or the Mantries or the activists or the people in powerful positions?

"Yeh unaka karttavy hai humaare prati"[15]

This is the need of the hour and a necessity for our generation.

---

15 It is their duty towards us.

Chapter 4

The New Generation

To see a level of jump in the economy, don't we all think that things need to change according to the requirements of the current generation? There should be a plan in action today to cater to the current changes in our society.

"Walk the walk of the generation."

The living cost if compared to the time when we got independence and today, there is a vast gap.

To fill this gap, the current generation needs help from the people in control. Their voices need to be heard. The ease of doing things should increase drastically in getting a job or doing business.

The struggling should stop. We could be in an illusion that change will not happen if we don't let it happen. Accepting that our cultures, our living standards, the cost of living, way of living and everything else are changing constantly is a start. We would be fools if we don't accept this.

The only solution we have is, improvising and changing the structures accordingly.

"System badalana padega"[16]

---

16 We need to change the system.

The Voice of the Current Generation

एक एहसास

ये वक्त का साया है जो मजबूर कर रहा।

ढूँढने को एक किनारा जो मिल न रहा।

ये जो पल हैं उनको खुशी का मौक़ा ना मिला।

जीत के कुछ लम्हे ढूँढने वाले को सहारा ना मिला।

आज निकला हूँ नया सवेरा लेके, कामियाबी की उम्मीद लेके, मैं बस इंतज़ार कर रहा।

बस इंतज़ार कर रहा।[17]

---

17 An emotion
The shadow of time which is compelling us.
We can't find a shore of hope and peace.
The times of happiness cannot find its way to an opportunity.
A person looking for success can't find his refuge.
I started my new beginning from this bright and gloom day, in a hope for new opportunity, but I am still just waiting for it.
Waiting for it

Chapter 5

The Solution

To every problem there is always a solution; my view is that there are numerous opportunities where we can all work together to work out the best plan for our state.

I have proposed some ideas in the further chapters of the book which could be considered to improve UP's system.

Everything is possible with just a will to do it.

> *"Galatiyon ko kamiyon ko kab tak chupate rahenge"*[18]
> *"Kuch na kuch toh karna hi padega"*[19]
> *"A company can fail, but a government cannot"*

I believe that the system which is present now was established by the British government as they didn't have enough British officers in the field to be deployed in just one country and their empire was so extensive. So, they enforced such a system where the power was distributed in such a way that control lied in the hands of just one person who at present times is known as the DM. (District Magistrate), which I believe is completely incorrect when we are seeing that the workload of just one person is so much so that mistakes tend to happen frequently. But we are not in that phase or age where we need to be

---

18 Till when will we keep hiding our mistakes and shortcomings?
19 We definitely need to do something.

ruled but we are in a stage where we need to improve. And I believe that we can achieve more if we work in a distributed manner.

Beautiful words from a person whom I dearly admire and it is my childhood wish to meet him someday; the chairman of the Tata group, Mr. Ratan Tata.

"If you want to walk fast, walk alone. But if you want to walk far, walk together."

– Ratan Tata

So, why do we still live in the British era?

Why?

I am not that person who is a waiting for changes to happen automatically but I am that person who will try to fix each one of them, for the betterment of my country and my people.

"When the world tries to bind you,
you make sure the leash is in your hands."

Chapter 6

Government Management Service

This will be an organisation that will look at the aspects of the government's working so that work is distributed and performed efficiently and at a much faster rate. A better management can bring out the best performance.

Roles/what will it do?

- Work force management: It means analysing all the departments where there is a need to hire new staff due to which there is a lag in the proceedings of the government officials. Or notice the basis of the workload where there is excess of staff and there is no need to have more staff at that place or position, with that analysis transferring them to other departments. In case, very less work is performed, merging the departments.

- Implementation of policies: Overlooking that all the policies which are implemented in the state are in action and monitoring them.

- Synchronisation with the Digital World:

  - Connecting with the digital world seems to be a necessary accomplishment. The documents from the past needs to be digitalised.

  - Checking and ensuring proper internet connectivity with the servers.

- o Checking and ensuring that all the digital documents are uploaded with the utmost accuracy in a particular time frame.

- o Digital training to the staff, with new updates on the website and software in all the departments to improve in the efficiency in working.

- o Collecting data from each department which includes a scorecard on efficient and fast working.

- o Changing the software on the basis of reports or demands of the information required or demanded from the public.

- o Supervising & training if given by private companies, in the process.

- o Improving various aspects of e-tendering on the basis of the feedback from the department and from the public.

- o Implementing the **Government Switch** platform where government officials post their resume, which is further discussed in the book.

- o Improving and enhancing data security and data breach from unauthorised access.

- Collecting feedbacks for the general public to improve in all the areas where the flow of work is slow or lagging.

- Findings the causes for delay or no delivery of results.

"Yeh Sab Chutkee bajane se nahi badalne wala hai"[20]

---

20   These things will not change with a snap of the fingers.

Working Structure

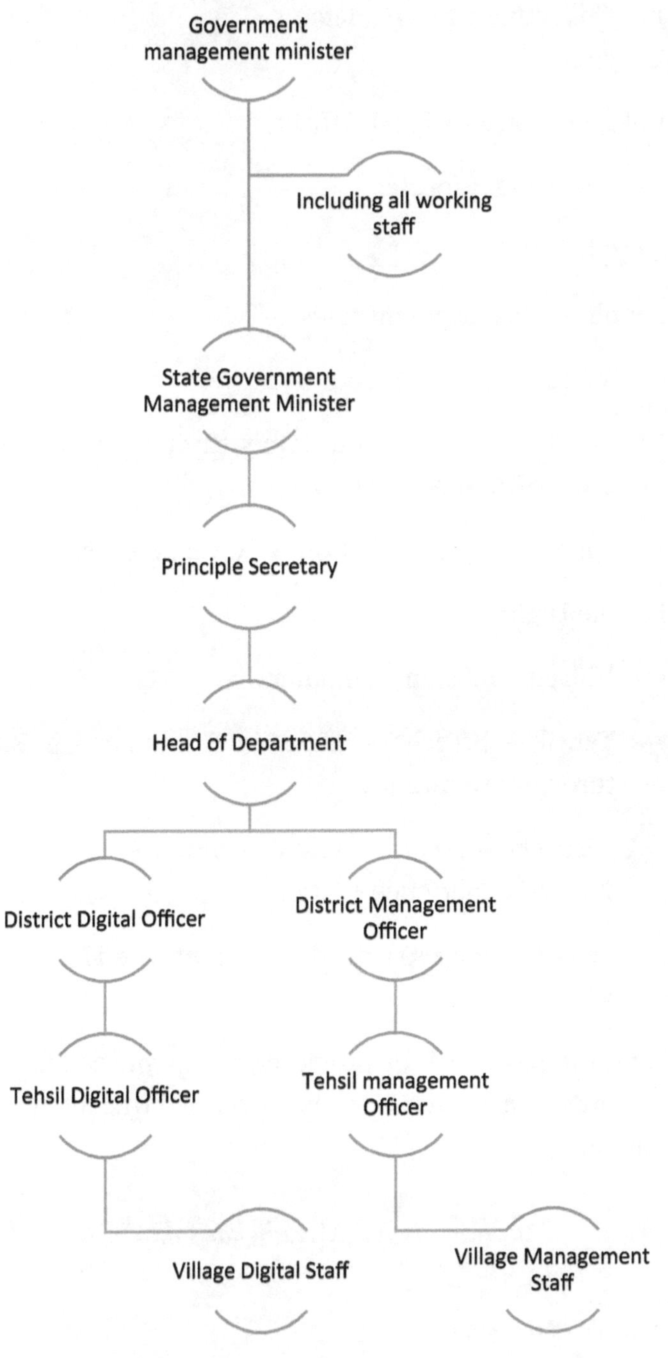

1. Roles of Management officer

   a. Workforce Management
   b. Collecting strategic data
   c. Analysis

2. Roles of District Digital Officer

   a. All Digital aspects.

Who can apply?

i. For all the management roles.

   - Village – BBA & B.Com

   - Tehsil – BBA & B.Com (Only through promotion) Direct only MBA or M.Com

   - District – MBA or M.Com + 10 years' experience + Exam

ii. For the Digital Roles

   - Village – B.Sc. in Computers

   - Tehsil – B.Tech or M.Sc. in Computers & B.Sc. (only through promotion)

   - District – M.Tech + 3 years' experience + Exam & B.Tech + 7 years' experience + Exam

Why is a there need for a separate department when NIC is doing the work already?

NIC is doing the basic task of providing things or facilitating things. Keeping records and analysis on the basis of efficient working is a different thing.

"Aur har kaam D.M. nahi kar sakta"[21]

---

21 DM cannot do all the work.

Chapter 7

The State Vision Fund

The State Vision Fund as the name suggests will cater to various segments of developments from social to economic or any other aspects associated. This fund will be used solely for development of the state for its better future. This should be mandatory for every state and especially for UP.

When we see ourselves we always have a vision. In the same manner we have a vision for our home, our society, our district, our state, our country; where we imagine that in a period of 10 years' time or 20 years' time the condition and the scenario of our state should change drastically and where we wish to see a new growth and a new opportunity for its people; where we see stable jobs, new businesses in the state, new infrastructure in the state, new sources of revenue, new digital infrastructure and new tourist destinations.

Like if we take an example from the project **Bhavy Vindhya Circuit** that we were working on with the honorable **Member of Parliament Sri Ram Shakal Ji**, we identified all the scenic spots, historical spots, places of worship, dams reservoirs of that region according to which we formulated a route map for the tourists who are visiting Varanasi so that these particular locations can also see exponential growth from the number of foreign and domestic tourists visiting our tourist circuit. In our project, we worked on plan where we identified which particular location should include what sort of tourist activity so that we make the tourist more involved in that destination and help them enjoy the scenic beauty of that place. By bringing in such projects for the state; could bring more & more revenue in the state.

These are the kind of tasks which the Vision Fund should involve itself to foresee the future of the state be it in the tourism sector, corporate sector, industrial sector and Infrastructure development. Basically involve its energy in bringing in the best possible future for its citizens and its country by constantly planning ahead of time.

> *"You want to have a future where you're expecting things to be better, not one where you're expecting things to be worse."*
>
> *– Elon Musk*

He is another visionary whom I dearly admire. He is the Founder of SpaceX, The Boring Company & X.com (now PayPal) and Co-founder of Tesla, Zip2, Neuralink & Chairman of SolarCity.

The future of the state holds for its citizens and that is what The Vision Fund is all about.

- Incubation of idea.

- Execution of idea.

- And all the necessary processes involved.

Roles

i.   Seeing the future aspects for the state.

ii. Involving all individuals involved to achieve that goal or target in hand.

iii. Making it in the form of a project.

iv. Planning the process of its execution.

v. Selling the idea to the public on the benefits of the project which holds for its citizens.

vi. Issuing Bonds if necessary (Discussed later).

vii. Allocating funds from various sources like the central fund, state fund, district fund and public fund which are required for the project.

Chapter 8

The State Vision Team

The State Vision Team will be involved rigorously in bringing a project from its incubation to final delivery. The team will involve people from various fields so as to promote ideas from every arena.

About the team

- Consist of 50 people of which 26 votes are needed to pass a project.

- In case of a tie, then the veto goes to the President of the team.

- Consisting of:

    ○ 25 Government officers.

    ○ 25 Businesses or people from different fields.

- Any member of the team is allowed to put up his or her idea on the table for review and vote.

The 25 Government individuals will involve:

- 2 – Members from the Ministry of the state.

- 1 – Member from the Central Ministry.

- 2 – Individuals from the PWD (Public Works Department).

- - 1 – Senior Member
  - 1 – Junior Member
- 2 – Individuals from the Irrigation Department.
  - 1 – Senior Member
  - 1 – Junior Member
- 2 – Individuals from Administration
  - 1 – Senior Member
  - 1 – Junior Member
- 1 – Member from the Forest Department
- 1 – Member from Excise Department
- 1 – Member from the Directorate of Geology and Mining
- 1 – Member from the Planning Department
- 1 – Member from the Agricultural Department
- 1 – Member from Housing & Urban Planning Department
- 1 – Member from Income Tax Department
- 1 – Member from G.S.T. Department (Goods & Services Tax)
- 1 – Member from Department of Medical Health &Family Welfare Department
- 1 – Member of the Education Department
- 1 – Member from the Government Department Retired with Experience
- 1 – Member from Government Management Service
- 1 – Member from State Tourism Department

- 1 – Member from the State Police Department

- 2 – Member from other state departments who could be shuffled accordingly

Note: Including Junior members as a main member is important as they know what is going around at the ground level so their feedback and ideas are important.

The 25 Private Individuals and Businesses will involve:

- 4 – Members from Major Manufacturing Units (All over India)

- 4 – Members from Major Manufacturing Units (All over the state)

- 2 – Members from Minor Manufacturing Units (All over from the State)

- 4 – Members from the Digital World or the IT Sector

- 2 – Members from the Startup Sector from the state

- 3 – Members from Various Businesses who are from Government Authorised Associations

- 1 – Member from Agricultural Association

- 1 – Member from Journalism

- 1 – Member from Tourism Industry

- 1 – Member from Film Industry

- 1 – Member from the Education Sector

- 1 – Member from Health Care Sector

All these members will put up in a project.

Propose a solution in the form of a presentation and present it to the team.

Whereas the public will contribute to

- 50% of the value to pass a project will come from the votes given by the public for the representation proposed as a project which is to be executed.

- The minimum number of public votes required to be considered to be counted in the process of passing a project would be 10,000.

- If the public votes do not qualify the 10,000 votes mark then the votes from the vision team will be the governing factor. This will only happen in a case where the team hasn't made much of an effort in making people aware about the project. In this case, an extension will be given by the team for making the people aware about the project. If after all that the numbers still come out to be less than 10,000 a review board will be assigned to look into it and approve.

- In case the votes against the project is 10 lakh or more than 75%, then the project is required to be amended or improved.

- Only 3 amendments are allowed to a project.

- Voting platform will be Government authorised platform only.

So, for a project to come into play in the state, 50% of the value comes from the Vision Team and 50% comes from the concerned or the affected public.

For the selection of the members initially, 5 temporary members will be appointed by the Chief Minister of the state.

- 2 – Members from engineering background.
  - Core engineering Departments
  - Work experience: more than 20 years

- ○ Post held: Chief Engineer and above

- ○ Best idea presented by them to the CM

- 2 – Members from the Administration background.

  - ○ 1 member from District Administration or the D.M.

  - ○ 1 Member from State Administration

  - ○ Work Experience: more than 20 years

  - ○ Best idea presented by them to the CM.

- 1 – Member from the Business Sector.

  - ○ More than 20 years of working within that state.

  - ○ Best idea Proposed to the CM.

- 5 – More candidates can be appointed if the CM feels Necessary.

  - ○ 2 – Direct members by the CM.

3 – Members could be appointed with the help of already selected.

They will be responsible for the formation of the team.

For the selection of the candidates from the government Departments, the government can implement and use a platform called Government Switch (Discussed later in the book) which is based on the number of projects they have completed and what idea they are willing to bring to the table.

"Always aim at perfection for only then will you achieve excellence."

– J.R.D Tata

He is the greatest gift to India. Major Industries and innovative developments happen due to his vision, in India.

Each Member to be a part of the team has to propose an idea to be a part of the team. **Stolen Ideas will not be accepted**. Need to have an authorisation from the particular individual or firm to represent it for approval by the team.

Every 2 years, new ideas are to be proposed by every member from the date of appointment or selection of that member.

> ➢ In case, there is no idea or representation within the 2-year period, an extension of six months will be given or else the member has to resign from the team.

The total term of the member will be 4 Years. A member can be re-elected or selected only for 3 terms.

In the case of a person who has completed his retirement, he can have the option to stay or leave the team.

So, who will be eligible to be the President?

- The Ministers i.e. state and central will not be eligible as they have plenty of work on their table. So, they will be taking part in the process of decision making and proposing any idea they have in mind.

- The individual who has proposed 5 or more projects or ideas of which minimum 1 has been passed by the team.

- The person can be elected only for a period of 3 years.

- The term of the individual can be only 2 times.

- The election will be carried out by the team and the public.

- The value of votes given by the team will be 51% and the value of votes given by the public through online process will be 49%.

- In the Initial stage of electing a person i.e. for the 1st president, 2 ideas are mandatory. The voting by the public accounts for 50% and the other 50% is by the selected members.

- In case of the vice president, a person who has proposed more than 7 ideas on the table of which minimum 1 of which is under consideration by the team.

- Various other responsibilities can be carried out by distributing it within the team, depending on their qualification.

Chapter 9

Business Development Department

The role of this department is to analyse the situation of the businesses in the state. Businesses are a major source of bread and butter for the mass population. So, the development of this sector becomes very vital.

"Businessman ke emotion ko samajho"[22]

Roles

- Creating a relationship or a bond between the businesses and the government.

- Based on business present in various districts. The initiatives which can be taken to improve the situation for a business.

- Analysing the potential of each district and what more can be done.

- Inviting and promoting each district as a hub or center of growth.

- Understanding the requirements of the businesses in terms of skilled labour for its growth. Ensuring ease of doing business and promoting the concept behind Make in India Initiative.

---

22 Understand the emotions of a businessman.

- Bringing in unregistered businesses to a suitable and do-able platform in which both the government and businesses can grow exponentially.

  - The UID or the Udyog Aadhar which is the Aadhar to all the businesses.

  - Giving them to the weaker business sectors such as the Thela's which includes fruit sellers, vegetable sellers, farmers and seasonal business owners to ensure a better economic result in the longer run.

To help this cause, the officers can go to each small or big organisation and register them. As the Thelawala's wouldn't be able to do it, help from this department would be a major boost in every industry.

  - To explain my point better, let us take an example of a Thelawala or roadside fruit seller who gets this unique ID (let's say Thela ID) which is already in place but the implementation which hasn't been done properly.

    - He would be eligible to get insurance.

    - Bank loan will be easily accessible, with the sales from his Thela.

    - Many opportunities and avenues will be open to him.

- Formation of registered Associations: That means that those associations can represent their issues and problems to the Business Development Officers from his or her area and from that feedback new and improved measures can be taken and it could be making new policies or any other initiatives.

  - Example:

    - Sabajiwala Association

    - Mutton & Chicken Seller Association

- o   Fruit Seller Association

- o   All small scale businesses Association

- o   All Major scale business association

So, grading of business can be done on the basis of their average income or type of business or the trade they are in.

Just to ensure there is no monopoly for the position of president in an association,

- o   No member can repeat two consecutive terms.

- o   Immediate family members also cannot participate in the second term if one of the family members was selected previously.

- Determining the districts which are famous for each industry.

- Development of 5 major and 5 small scale industries which can be setup in a particular district (Discussed later in the book).

- These will be the industries for which the government will give major subsidy or benefits such as Business Establishment Funds to.

- Various other industries can also be setup. But all of the determined industries will be given the first preference as they will be the main industry in the district.

- Some of the options for industries which can be established are:

  - ➢   Electronics

  - ➢   AI. (Artificial Intelligence)

  - ➢   Arms and Ammunition

  - ➢   Space Research

> ➢ Film production

> ➢ Aviation

> ➢ Automobile

> ➢ Tourism

> ➢ Gaming, etc.

- To promote liberalisation and globalisation.

- Understanding the demand of the generation.

- Changing business policies.

- Understanding which tax criteria, a particular business fits in.

- Checking on illegal practices if any executed by any particular industry.

- Connecting and transitioning all the industries towards a digital and secure platform.

- Just to ensure that a sector never fails or the industry never fails; constant training and support given by the government to the staff and its owners from the market leaders from that particular industry in each district.

- Marketing and promotion responsibility of the products produced in those industries, by the department internationally and nationally.

Working Structure

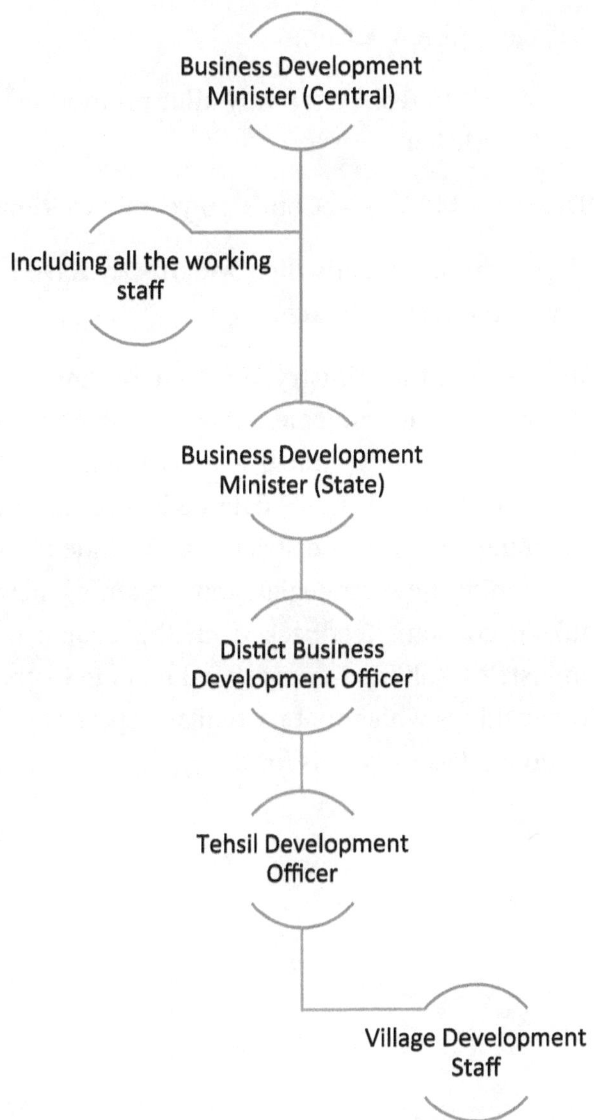

Recruitment process

- Conducting Government Exam

- Who can apply?
  - Village – BBA & B.Com
  - Tehsil – BBA & B.Com (Only after promotion) Direct only MBA & M.Com.
  - District – MBA or M.Com + 10 years' experience + Exam

Why is this department needed when we already have the Ministry of Commerce and Industry in place?

It is because the ministry of commerce and industry is just involved in the implementation of the policies and other things related to it. But this department will be involved in doing so much more data collection in every district, planning for each district as an independent entity, developing new strategies, implementing new strategies, taking constant feedback from the people from various industries, solving issues related to an industry and lots of other things which that particular department is incapable of doing. Basically, it is for doing all the groundwork.

Chapter 10

Education

The current scenario of education that we see is that of people not understanding the concept and just copying what has been written word to word.

Most of us who have reached various positions in our country are just copying artists. There are very few brilliant minds that are thinking or planning towards innovation or changing the scenario. So, we can presently see the state of our country which is completely based on copying what other countries are doing.

Yes, we are noticing a few changes in the industry after a long time but there is room for a major change in the industry and more room for innovation. Yes, there is a sense which is coming to the society which is thinking in this direction which we can see in the IT sector and its sudden boom. Practical learning, I believe is the way to go now.

Making major pieces into little bits of pieces, enables more room for learning, creative thinking and exploring the particular.

Let me give you an example to understand my point. What actually happens when you copy?

The correct Statement:

Ram's wife gave birth to a beautiful child Bramha.

The state of the person who understood the statement made up his own statement with the same meaning: -

The wife of Ram gave birth to a beautiful child Bramha.

The person who copied the statement forgot just one word:

Ram gave birth to a beautiful child Bramha.

Is this the type of leaning that should be acceptable?

What if the person who checks the copy doesn't notice the missing word?

Is this the kind of person we are willing to bring to our society?

Are we willing to take that risk?

There is one word to describe them.

Rattu - Tota.[23]

So, it might happen that the person in position and power could be or become a *Rattu – Tota* officer.

This in real sense if you see will be a disaster for the society, right?

---

23   A Copying parrot.

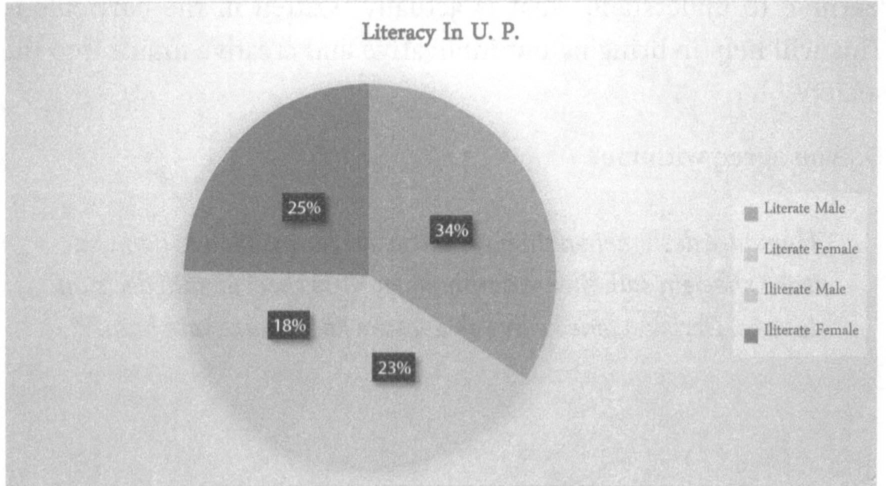

Based on the Census of U.P. in 2011

What may be happening or might happen?

> The policies, statements, letters and documents presented to them could not be understood which in turn would result in no implementation or an incorrect implementation.

So, the bigger picture says that are we bringing *Rattu – Totas'* into our world. We don't want a disaster to happen and collapse everything around us.

Things need to change in our learning process and the shift should be towards practical learning in every sense to build concept-based learning to understand what is actually written in the curriculum. This will help in bringing out innovative and creative minds into the society.

Do you agree with me?

> *"Humaare desh mein abhi naye initiative lene vaalon ki kami hai, jisako cheejein samajh me aarahi ho aur uss cheej pe sahi decision le sake. Decision lene ke liye ek doosare ka munh takate hain."*[24]

---

24 We have a scarcity of people who are willingly to take an initiativeand those who can also understand things and will take the right decisions. But sadly, today we see each other's faces to take the right decision.

Off topic

The people who are good speakers may or may not always have the best knowledge about the concerned topic. I generally love to read a person who is talking to me. I read their body language, what they speak, how they behave. I improve my knowledge about a person and try to understand what is actually going on inside their heads. I read somewhere that at times you need to pretend to be a fool in front of a fool. I personally recommend, listen more and speak less. Maybe he might have 98% of non-sense in what he says but between those lines he might end up saying 2% of something that has value and substance which could become an asset to you. Observe and absorb.

If I look at any person in power, it could be an officer, politician, or anybody as a matter of fact, he will always know and completely know all the wrong or harmful powers and never know all the good powers. He will not completely know what good he could bring to the society.

"Knowledge is power and power is everything."

If you possess either of them, people will flock around you. You will see nobody coming and flocking around a person who has no power or has no knowledge.

What do you take away from the world?
Is it money or property?
You only take your fixed asset which is knowledge.
"Sirf aur sirf aap apni knowledge leke jaatee hain, jiski vajah se aapko duniya yaad rakhegi"[25]

---

25   The only thing that you take from this world is the knowledge you had and only that will be the reason why the people will remember you.

Chapter 11

What Comes out Must Stay in

What comes out must stay in, if we break this sentence and understand it, and then it means that whatever trade, business, profession we are in, we earn a certain amount from that profession, right? That could be salary, profit or various other sources of income. So, this is actually what is coming **OUT** from our hard work in our profession. The next phrase, "Must stay in" means that whatever amount we earn should stay in this very country or in that particular state for its economic growth.

Let's think of this in this manner with an example:

That a person of 25 years of age earns 45,000 rupees per month plans a trip to Dubai using his savings, which cost him Rs. 1,25,000 for his entire journey which includes his hotel, stay and everything in his itinerary as well as his purchases in that country.

But what it means for a country as a whole?

It clearly means that a loss of Rs. 1, 25,000 has occurred for the entire country. That's just from just one individual, so see the population of our country and you can guess a number to estimate, to what extent the country is in loss.

What does it mean in the case of a state?

Let us say, that very individual planned a trip to Goa, and then his total trip will now cost him 75,000 rupees. Now most of us will think that the money has stayed inside our country and that is very good. But sadly, no, that is not what it will mean for a state. Let us say that the individual belongs to the state of UP and he spends his money in Goa. Then in this case the state of UP incurred a loss of Rs. 75,000 which is a loss in the revenue of the state.

> *"Monitor the cash flow constantly,*
> *to adapt to that environment gradually."*

So, do I mean we should stop spending or investing money in other countries or states?

No, what I mean is that a balance has to be made between the money which is going out and money coming in.

Did you Know?
The Indian tourists are among the world's highest spenders per visit made abroad, with visitor' spending expected to increase from USD 23 billion in 2018 to USD 45 billion by 2022.

How?

We can do this by increasing the sources of revenue which will help in boosting our economy, right? That is necessary at the moment as we are currently experiencing a major drop in our economy after various plans executed by the government and the spread of COVID-19 which is also not helping us in anyway and leading us into a financial crash.

> *"Ek desh ki economy bachane ke liye hume ye dekhna hoga ki, paisa*
> *na humaare Desh se jyaada jaaye aur na uss Pradesh se jahaan*
> *usaka janam hua hai."*[26]

So, basic economics says that workis needed to be done towards bringing the money into the country and the state.

> *"Generation se haath milao"*[27]

---

26 For the progress of a country we need to make sure that the money generated from the country and the state where it was initially generated goes out from there.

27 Shake hands with the generation.

Chapter 12

The Black Economy

Everyone is aware of the term Black Money, right?

But do we really?

The unregistered income under circulation in any circumstances can be considered as a part of the Black Income.

The inclusion of all the population who are working in an unregistered environment who are generating black income which in turn results in the formation of a parallel Black Economy.

What does it mean? Let us take an example for you to understand this concept better.

A person has an income of 25,000 rupees from his job for which he pays taxes. In his house, he has two rooms which earn him 5000 rupees each. So, the total rental income amounts to 10,000 rupees. He tutors 3 students after work which earns him an additional amount of 8,000. So, to put things in perspective the amount of black income generated by that very person becomes 18,000 rupees cash each month. His monthly expense including everything comes out to be around 35,000 rupees. The rest he saves for his family and any future endeavours. Every month 6 -7 thousand is spent on a ration which includes daily necessary things such as vegetable, rice, lentils, etc. Out of which most of it is paid in cash. The amount which is paid in cash let us say to the vegetable seller or to the ration store. The store or the seller pays to his supplier and the supplier pays to the farmer.

All is good till now?

The farmer then buys a land which costs him 1, 10,000 rupees but the registered cost for that land is just 45,000 rupees and the rest is paid in cash to the previous owner. So, you can observe that it is a chain reaction that resulted in the formation of a larger amount.

"Motivate a person to put his money in the banks and
pay taxes on it."

So, in this case the extra income which was floated can be termed under black income. This extra which is not taxed is termed as Black Income.

But does that mean it was earned without involving any hard work?

No.

When this money floats around, then this becomes Black Money.

Yes, corruption is a major source of black income but if you see the larger picture it's the combination of all the unregistered incomes which result in the formation of a Parallel Economy which is the Black Economy.

"Apne faayade ke liye hum corrupt hain, wese to hame pata hi nahi
ki corruption hota kya hai."[28]

---

28   For the benefit of ourselves we all are corrupt, or else we wouldn't have known what corruption is.

Chapter 13

What is Illegal, Should be Made Legal

Major chunks of money which floats illegally should be made legal to regularise and restrict a person involved in it in too much or at risk and we know that it will happen no matter how many efforts we put in to bring it down.

What I mean is that everyone knows sports betting are the most favourite thing in India of which cricket comes out to be on top. Other illegal activities going on a massive scale in India are gambling, drugs & prostitution which I guess is not something that could easily be acceptable. I think legalising these activities this could be a step towards reducing the amount of rape that happens in this country. No one can change the mindset of a rapist but think about the scenario where he has an option to go to instead. I think it is a topic for another day. Yes, it might hinder our age old cultural ethics but I don't think it is bigger than the issue of rape. These are just my point of views that you may differ from, but for me this seems to be the right step in the right direction.

So, coming back to illegal businesses such as gambling, any kind of betting, some less harmful drugs served in a specified quantity in a regularised and monitored manner and various other businesses which might run illegally which take a chunk out from our economy, would help boost our economy.

This could be an opportunity for the growth for the government.

A solution to this could be where we legalise these business ventures in a controlled and monitored environment where a person would rather pay taxes on it and have an earning from these sources. Imagine then, where our economy would rise.

Did you Know?
The Indian gambling market is estimated to be worth USD60 billion per year.

Example:

If a person earns from betting or gambling, impose 38% or 28% GST or maximum tax which seems fit. And if that person's earning which is an amount, let us say equal to X, then he can't invest more than 40% of his earnings in that venture in a particular financial year.

In a case where he has invested more than 40%, he would have to pay up more taxes and also justify that his family finances were running smoothly and that he has not incurred any dept.

In some cases, we all might have heard or observed where a person got himself so much involved in these quick and easy ways of making money that at times they realise that recovery from it for his family seems like a disaster.

In the case of drugs not including synthetic drugs but yes, some common drugs which are in use, it could be a possibility a certain amount or quantity could be procured from a legalised store by showing a Government-issued ID (Could be Aadhar or specific ID for it). In this way the government would know the quantity of drugs which are being floated across the country and taken by its citizens. It's earnings can be used to promote the advertisements which involves showing what harms it could do to the body as in the case of alcohol and cigarettes that is in a certain month, this much quantity is permitted to a person on that particular ID.

In this case also there will be black marketing by the people who are not taking drugs and people who are using excessive drugs. But the quantity and its sales will be known to the government which could help them in reducing the number of citizens using or consuming them.

The benefits of legalising this are that it will boost the economy. An opportunity for growth in these business sectors in a monitored form and prevent massive illegal trade. And this will help in reducing taxes on various daily necessary commodities.

More tax means more money can float around in the development of our country in various sectors.

If you see Nepal, Malaysia, Singapore, Thailand, Dubai, Amsterdam and other countries, they are basically running these ventures legally and their economy is solely dependent on these sources of income.

Nepal, a neighbouring country of ours is functioning because of Indian tourists going and spending their cash on a gambling spree which makes a major dent in our economy.

"Source. Resource. Conquer."

Chapter 14

The State Stock Exchange

As there is plenty of scope in every state especially UP, we could introduce a stock exchange in every state.

As the Bombay stock exchange and national stock are for those companies that are in the market and have a paid-up capital of 10 crore rupees or more. This helps them in achieving great heights in that particular sector by acquiring new investors, helping them in having a better future for the company.

In case of a state we could drop that number down to Rupees 5 crore or less whichever amount seems best for that state as the paid-up capital. The amount of paid-up capital could vary according to the economic condition of the state. This way a state could bring in more investors from within the state or across the globe which will help a company establish itself on a global scale.

In the field of startups, we could introduce a separate platform in the exchange of a state itself where a startup can raise the capital for its idea or company. And put up his project or idea to be seen by the startup investors on the stock exchange platform.

This platform will inform the following for the investors:

- Basic idea of the startup

- Strategy for its growth

- Initiatives taken by the Entrepreneur

- Market implementation and its marketing strategy

- Basic costs involved throughout the process

- Details of a project or a report about the startup

In such a case if a startup gets registered in the State Startup Stock Exchange (SSSE) platform, the investors will get an annual registration done and take a pledge that they will not be associated or involved in copy of any idea or project being listed in the investor's forum.

Suppose a company wishes to establish a business franchise in the state and is planning a major project or even the government is planning a project. What could be done is that the money can be invested by its citizens of the particular state also.

Let's say:

An FDI is supposed to happen in our country by a very major firm or an Indian firm wishes to expand and setup in UP.

It should be mandatory for a company to issue 40% of the value of its project to be listed in the state stock exchange. Or the company should be traded in the state in terms of stocks or shares and bonds.

"Initial cost toh lagegee hi, us company ko setup hone mein.
Aur profit jo hoga woh bhi logon tak pahunch jaega in the form
of interest or dividend"[29]

Or in case of the government; to explain this let's take an example:

Let us say an Express Highway is decided to be built in a particular state. It is estimated that the cost of the project is 1, 200 crore rupees

---

29   There will always be an initial cost for setting up an industry which could be eased from the public investment. And later the public can earn on that investment from interest or dividends.

for the state & central government but they can spare or spend only 600 crore rupees. So what happens is that it takes out a loan from the World Bank.

What will happen now?

In this case, the government will be paying an extra amount as interest to the World Bank which makes the cash flow statement say that the money is going out of our country.

Is this cash flow Good or bad?

I guess anyone who has taken a loan ever in their lifetime must be aware of the fact that we need to pay the principal amount as well as the interest amount to the bank. Here, what is happening is that the extra amount which is the interest is being paid by our government that is floated internationally.

Should we stop borrowing loans from the World Bank?

No.

My solution is that for any project, the 40% stakeholders should be its citizens, giving first preference to the citizens of the state in the first round. If the required amount is not achieved, then it should be floated inside the country. Then the World Bank should come into picture.

"Taki Desh ka paisa Desh me hi rahe,
Logon ko usse faayada bhi ho"[30]

What can the government do?

For a particular project the government can issue Bonds for 40% of the total amount. That could be of small amounts so that the government

---

30   So that our country's money stays in our country and the public also benefits from that money.

can have more and more people investing in them. As we all know the fact that those bonds pay you interest.

The benefit to this is that the loan is taken by the government from its citizens on which the government pays interest.

Let's head back to the same example:

So, for the project government could spare only Rupees 600 crores out of the total amount of Rupees 1200 crores. Let's say that out of the 1200 crores 40% is now being invested by the citizens of our country in terms of Bonds which amounts to be Rupees 480 crores which is achieved in two or three rounds. And now what is left can be acquired from the World Bank which amounts to be Rupees 120 crores.

Let's say if the total amount which was left and could not be fulfilled by our government was taken from the World Bank at an interest rate of 9.5% (which was in 2018 for India) for a period of 10 years.

How much extra money are we paying?

You can calculate that number by yourself. Understand how it will impact our economy. And how much interest we are paying to the World Bank. Yes, we are paying from our very own taxes.

"Sarkar ka paisa hai hame usse kya?"[31]

Even if the government pays 6% or 7% or even lesser amount as interest to its citizens, still both the parties will be happy. As the government is paying low interest for that amount and the people are making money from the money which was just sitting in the banks. The government can give tax benefits to its citizens in these types of investments by its people.

The same is applicable for a state.

---

31   That is the government's money, not ours. Why should we be concerned?

"Jab humaara paisa lagega toh farak padega. Aur paisa laga ke kaam nikalvaane mein toh hum Hindustani maahir hain"[32]

Statement of a common man:

"Aree Sarkar ko kis baat ki kami hai, bahut paisa hai."[33]
"Bahut paisa hota toh tax kyun badhaatee jo ki bewakoofon ki tarah hum bharte hain"[34]

Sarkar:

"Funds kahaan se laen, ek kaam karo tax rate badhado"[35]

What is the Government's source of income?

Taxes.

Why does a government need to take a loan?

To understand this let's take an example:

A person of an age 30 decides to construct a room and a bathroom in his house for himself and his family. He will require funds. Let us say that the person has a total savings of 3 lakh rupees. The estimated cost required for the construction of a room and bathroom in his house is 2 lakh rupees. Takes out 1 lakh rupees from his savings and for the rest of the amount, he takes a loan i.e. 1 lakh rupees for a period of 3 years.

Why did he take a loan when he already had money in his account?

---

32 When our money will be invested then we will definitely be affected. We Indians are experts in getting the work done if our hard earned money is invested.
33 Government has no issues of money, they have a lot of it.
34 If government had a lot of money, then why would they increase the tax rates? Then we would be fools complying to the increase in tax rates.
35 How are we going to manage the funds? Let's increase the tax rate.

It is because he has family expenses every month which may exceed at times in case of education fees for his kids, travel expenses, the requirement of food due to guests coming to his place and in case of a medical emergency. That would be a logical thing to do. Don't you agree?

So, that's the reason why the government takes a loan also. But it's important to access only the right amount of loan which is to be taken. So, it is important to manage the funds which we have and is to be taken as loan. Taking excessive loans is also not good and taking a lesser amount of loans is also not good. Hitting the Right figure is crucial.

"We need to crack the code of economy together or we might fail in the long run."

Tell me,

Now who loves or even likes to pay taxes on their hard-earned incomes?

Tell you what.

Not even the people working in that very department or ministry.

"Hum toh aam insaan hain. Hume humari income pe tax kyun dena pasand aaega. woh toh majbooree hojaatee hai ki pay karna hai"[36]

---

36   We are just common people. Why would we want to pay tax on the income we have from our hard work? It becomes compulsory for us to pay.

Chapter 15

The State Fund Management Team

The team as the name suggests would be responsible for allocating funds and managing funds for the state and the country.

Why call it a team and not a department?

It is because when a small number of people come together, the efforts of every person count in achieving a particular goal or target and we accomplish it efficiently. It makes sense to call it a team. In the case of a department, what I feel is, it sounds more like a laid-back job where nobody wishes to work and is waiting for their salary to be credited. But still, when the workload for a team seems to get bigger, we should establish a department. And government organisations are always known to be departments. The number of people employed in that particular place is more so the work can be divided. I clearly do not mean that every department has the same feeling. There are many people in every department doing an honest man's work.

Why is it important?

If a project is thought of and it is to be executed by any government department, analysis of the amount of funds required by calculating the estimated cost of the task or project is done. On the basis of which, the amount that would be needed from the state government, central government and the district will be decided. After that, determining how much money can be taken from the public is done (by issuing bonds, stocks, etc.) and the remaining which is to be borrowed from various other sources, one of which is the World Bank.

Roles

- Analyse the project in hand

- Procurement of funds

  - District

  - State

  - Country

  - Outside the country

- Phases in which the money is required

- Management of the money which is been taken from the various sources

- Checking and rechecking the flow of cash and how it is being spent

- Amount of work done with that money

Did you Know?
The Uttar Pradesh government presented a 4.79 lakh crore rupees budget for 2019–20. How much of it was really used?

The team must comprise of:

1. Investment banker

2. Qualified Engineers

3. Qualified in Management courses

4. Government representatives from that particular project

5. Stock and Market analyst

All the funds should go through this team. If the funds remain unused, they will be responsible and answerable to the government and the public. The results of each year shall be presented publicly so that each passing year would ensure more and more progress by improvising and improving its processes and structures.

Chapter 16

The State Project Management Team

This team decides what projects are necessary, what should be executed from the period of its incubation to its final stage which launches the project for the public. Ensuring funds which are required by estimating its cost is also its primary role. Timely delivery of the project in various stages of payments is ensured and that work is being delivered, making sure that there are no hiccups to achieve a particular deadline.

> *"All the powers in the universe are already ours. It is we who have put our hands before our eyes and cry that it is dark."*
>
> *– Swami Vivekananda*

- Analysis of every data regarding the project coming from any and every department.

- Analysis of market rates and scheduled rates for the payments of a particular task is appropriate.

- Synchronisation between the fund and the project efficiency.

- E-tendering process should be done by this team for every department of the state.

Roles

- Analysing every data regarding the project.

- E-tendering for every department.

- All the Project management roles

  - Activity and Resource Planning

  - Monitoring progress

  - Organising and motivating the team responsible for the completion of that task or project

  - Controlling time management

  - Cost estimating and developing the budget

  - Analysing and managing project risk

  - Managing reports and necessary documentation

The team must comprise of:

1. Qualified Engineers

2. Qualified in Management courses

3. Government representatives from the particular departments

4. Private consultants only if necessary

Why is it necessary?

It is important as the current status for a long time, of our country has been the status quo due to various hiccups at various levels in most of the government organisations so as to improve the quality and efficiency.

Chapter 17

Government Switch

It is a platform where government officers can post their resume and switch to various other departments or government organisations. So, what that means is that an official will work in a certain department and will retire from the same department only if he builds a strong resume during his service period.

This platform will even help the government in choosing the best candidates based on their performance.

"Ek samay tha jab Hindustan ko puri duniya,
Sone ki chidiya keh kar bulaatee thi"[37]

Main focus of this platform is:

1. Performance

2. Efficiency of work or efficient working

3. Credibility of a candidate

4. Performance-based promotion

If a candidate is recruited in a certain department, the minimum duration to use this particular opportunity of Government Switch facility is 3 years. This is so that he gains minimum experience.

---

37   There was a time when India was called the golden bird.

Let us take an example:

A government job aspirant gives the UPSC exam in which he gets selected in P W D. (Public Works Department). To gain experience he works there for 3 years. Based on his performance during those 3 years, it would be decided, if he will stay or work in another department or in a case where he wishes to apply to another department. The government will see his or her report card where the available information regarding the candidate is present as the number of projects completed, the number of new projects initiated, the number of files completed and number of cases closed. It also includes the number of government initiatives executed and various other important factors.

"Ab mantriyon ki chaatane ki zaroorat nahi padegi"[38]

This resume will be present in the government digital portal where this information is present based on which government can automate this process (through AI in the coming future). This is done in the form of deputation and points but this processing is too slow and inefficient due to various factors present in the department and the involvement of ministry in some cases.

"Ab kaam karoge tabhi naam kamaoge"

So, now with the performance graph present, he or she can apply for various positions in India from Kashmir to Kanyakumari in the state or central governments.

If they feel that the candidate is indispensable for the department; the department can put a veto for the candidate. But will have to give that candidate an appraisal or incentive.

---

38   Now the government employee need not have to request or depend on ministers for job postings or in case of recruitment.

This will help in analysing workforce needed also, that if a certain department needs more helping hands to complete their tasks on time or if a certain department needs less staff due to lack of work. In a case where the work is very less and could be executed under a parent department then merging the departments can also be done.

It is possible that there are areas where there is more amount of work and areas where there is less amount of work, so how will we get to the conclusion about the candidate if he or she is fit to go to a particular department or not. In that case ratio between the amount of work to the work completed and to the time frame in which the work was performed would be helpful.

The Ratio:

Amount of Work: Work Completed: Time Frame

This ratio when calculated will get us the right candidate for a particular job.

Do you agree if this is implemented, we will get the best results out of everyone?

> *"Jo kaam karta hai aur jo usaka credit leta hai do alag-alag baaten hain."*[39]
> *"Ab ussi ka naam goonjega, jo kaam kar ke dekhayega"*[40]

To reduce work Apprentice and Internship programmes can be introduced where the amount of work is more and the requirement of more candidates seems necessary or more trained candidates are required for that line of work.

---

39 The person who works hard for a particular work and the person who takes credit of his work are two different things.

40 Now the people will know the name of only that person who is willing to work hard for it.

Chapter 18

Policy Formation & Review Board

This organisation will basically work on the policies, agenda, initiatives, Yojanas and various other documents that are responsible for governing a department; either improving them or making a fresh one on the basis of its need.

This organisation will do is work on policies or agendas which were made decades back and improve or remove them if they think that it is obsolete. Various parts are still present in the government policies which are no longer relevant for the society and the people involved in that line of work.

I recently read a beautiful line from the Prince of Udaipur, a direct descendent of a great warrior Maharana Pratap.

"The idea is not to prove, but improve."

– Lakshyaraj Singh Mewar

This line holds a deeper meaning to it not just for an individual but for an organisation and for a government like ours which desperately needs to think in this direction. That is indicating us to improve and change to bring a new revolution in our country.

Why are we still holding on to things from the past generation?

In every five years, all the points of the policies or agendas from every department or organisation should be reviewed by this board on the findings and demand to improve the current generation's requirements.

To the board's use, putting every document or policy to a digital platform that every individual can access and according to his perspective what changes could be made to the current policy can be suggested by sharing his ideas on the portal to help the organisation in improving. Private firms can also help the government in the formation or reformation of any policy which seems necessary. If any change is required; bring digital voting into perspective which would allow its citizens to participate in this process.

How will it be executed?

The board will divide itself into teams that will look into various sectors. Then the particular team will upload that particular policy or document which is under review and under their supervision which would be accessible to the citizens on the online portal. If a citizen wishes to recommend a change in that portal, he or she will select the policy online and then select the paragraph or point where he or she is recommending the change. Then he will write down his points of recommendation. Then that part or paragraph goes to vote by the general public as well as the board.

At the end of each policy, the officer who has read the paragraph or points from each portion should be mentioned. And the date when it was last reviewed should also be mentioned.

Chapter 19

The Districts

In UP, how many districts are there? Can you guess?

There are 75 districts in the state of Uttar Pradesh and these districts desperately need a doctor who could solve all the issues which are present in the district. To help them generate more revenue and reduce the unemployment rate. This should be planned in such a way, that the basic sole of each district remains intact.

The following are the districts in the state of Uttar Pradesh:

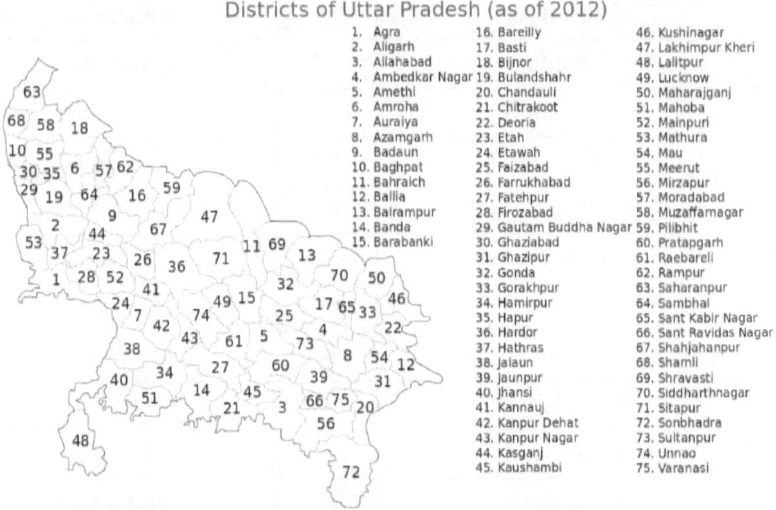

Image Sourced from Wikipedia

List of districts in Uttar Pradesh			
Sr. No.	District	Sr. No.	District
1	Agra	39	Jaunpur
2	Aligarh	40	Jhansi
3	Ambedkar Nagar	41	Kannauj
4	Amethi (ChatrapatiSahujiMahraj Nagar)	42	Kanpur Dehat
5	Amroha (J.P. Nagar)	43	Kanpur Nagar
6	Auraiya	44	Kanshiram Nagar (Kasganj)
7	Ayodhya	45	Kaushambi
8	Azamgarh	46	Kushinagar (Padrauna)
9	Baghpat	47	Lakhimpur - Kheri
10	Bahraich	48	Lalitpur
11	Ballia	49	Lucknow
12	Balrampur	50	Maharajganj
13	Banda	51	Mahoba
14	Barabanki	52	Mainpuri
15	Bareilly	53	Mathura
16	Basti	54	Mau
17	Bhadohi	55	Meerut
18	Bijnor	56	Mirzapur
19	Budaun	57	Moradabad
20	Bulandshahr	58	Muzaffarnagar
21	Chandauli	59	Pilibhit
22	Chitrakoot	60	Pratapgarh
23	Deoria	61	Prayagraj
24	Etah	62	Raebareli

25	Etawah	63	Rampur
26	Farrukhabad	64	Saharanpur
27	Fatehpur	65	Sambhal (Bhim Nagar)
28	Firozabad	66	Sant Kabir Nagar
29	Gautam Buddha Nagar	67	Shahjahanpur
30	Ghaziabad	68	Shamali (Prabuddh Nagar)
31	Ghazipur	69	Shravasti
32	Gonda	70	Siddharth Nagar
33	Gorakhpur	71	Sitapur
34	Hamirpur	72	Sonbhadra
35	Hapur (Panchsheel Nagar)	73	Sultanpur
36	Hardoi	74	Unnao
37	Hathras	75	Varanasi
38	Jalaun		

Initially we need to get the facts and figures of the district in place to help understand what the growth opportunities in that particular district are. The natural resources which are present; the cultural heritage of that district, connectivity to major cities, unemployment rate, institutions present, major or small industries present in that area, sports and various amenities, tourist facilities, health care facilities, etc. are present.

Do you know what the Unemployment rate was in the Census of 2011 of U.P.?

It was when I researched and found the data on the census that I would find out that it was **67%.**

Can you believe it?

Yes, we all can because it is UP, so, it is a possible number for UP.

The following data will give you a better idea on the subject:

Based on the Census in 2011							
SR. NO.	DISTRICT	LEVEL	NAME	TRU	TOTAL WORKING POPULATION	NON-WORKING POPULATION	UNEMPLOYMENT RATE
	0	STATE	UTTAR PRADESH	Total	65814715	133997626	67%
1	132	DISTRICT	Saharanpur	Total	1037344	2429038	70%
2	133	DISTRICT	Muzaffarnagar	Total	1291644	2851868	69%
3	134	DISTRICT	Bijnor	Total	1088036	2594677	70%
4	135	DISTRICT	Moradabad	Total	1417811	3354195	70%
5	136	DISTRICT	Rampur	Total	737261	1598558	68%
6	137	DISTRICT	JyotibaPhule Nagar	Total	599089	1241132	67%
7	138	DISTRICT	Meerut	Total	1090539	2353150	68%
8	139	DISTRICT	Baghpat	Total	416695	886353	68%
9	140	DISTRICT	Ghaziabad	Total	1520538	3161107	68%
10	141	DISTRICT	Gautam Buddha Nagar	Total	569109	1079006	65%
11	142	DISTRICT	Bulandshahr	Total	1173260	2325911	66%
12	143	DISTRICT	Aligarh	Total	1174361	2499528	68%
13	144	DISTRICT	Mahamaya Nagar	Total	484115	1080593	69%

14	145	DISTRICT	Mathura	Total	840939	1706245	67%
15	146	DISTRICT	Agra	Total	1389844	3028953	69%
16	147	DISTRICT	Firozabad	Total	761521	1736635	70%
17	148	DISTRICT	Mainpuri	Total	560840	1307689	70%
18	149	DISTRICT	Budaun	Total	1107343	2574553	70%
19	150	DISTRICT	Bareilly	Total	1401971	3046388	68%
20	151	DISTRICT	Pilibhit	Total	618605	1412402	70%
21	152	DISTRICT	Shahjahanpur	Total	892214	2114324	70%
22	153	DISTRICT	Kheri	Total	1264718	2756525	69%
23	154	DISTRICT	Sitapur	Total	1422602	3061390	68%
24	155	DISTRICT	Hardoi	Total	1318946	2773899	68%
25	156	DISTRICT	Unnao	Total	1124744	1983623	64%
26	157	DISTRICT	Lucknow	Total	1542806	3047032	66%
27	158	DISTRICT	Rae Bareli	Total	1204710	2200849	65%
28	159	DISTRICT	Farrukhabad	Total	592267	1292937	69%
29	160	DISTRICT	Kannauj	Total	524676	1131940	68%
30	161	DISTRICT	Etawah	Total	506072	1075738	68%
31	162	DISTRICT	Auraiya	Total	442023	937522	68%
32	163	DISTRICT	Kanpur Dehat	Total	628864	1167320	65%
33	164	DISTRICT	Kanpur Nagar	Total	1572232	3009036	66%
34	165	DISTRICT	Jalaun	Total	620764	1069210	63%

Continued...

35	166	DISTRICT	Jhansi	Total	814914	1183689	59%
36	167	DISTRICT	Lalitpur	Total	503351	718241	59%
37	168	DISTRICT	Hamirpur	Total	443655	660630	60%
38	169	DISTRICT	Mahoba	Total	349676	526282	60%
39	170	DISTRICT	Banda	Total	701689	1097721	61%
40	171	DISTRICT	Chitrakoot	Total	394197	597533	60%
41	172	DISTRICT	Fatehpur	Total	1063929	1568804	60%
42	173	DISTRICT	Pratapgarh	Total	1066601	2142540	67%
43	174	DISTRICT	Kaushambi	Total	639086	960510	60%
44	175	DISTRICT	Allahabad	Total	2111907	3842484	65%
45	176	DISTRICT	Bara Banki	Total	1192850	2067849	63%
46	177	DISTRICT	Faizabad	Total	831209	1639787	66%
47	178	DISTRICT	Ambedkar Nagar	Total	787398	1610490	67%
48	179	DISTRICT	Sultanpur	Total	1242632	2554485	67%
49	180	DISTRICT	Bahraich	Total	1152160	2335571	67%
50	181	DISTRICT	Shrawasti	Total	403755	713606	64%
51	182	DISTRICT	Balrampur	Total	760253	1388412	65%
52	183	DISTRICT	Gonda	Total	1170552	2263367	66%
53	184	DISTRICT	Siddharthnagar	Total	878898	1680399	66%
54	185	DISTRICT	Basti	Total	783688	1680776	68%

55	186	DISTRICT	Sant Kabir Nagar	Total	539469	1175714	69%
56	187	DISTRICT	Mahrajganj	Total	994253	1690450	63%
57	188	DISTRICT	Gorakhpur	Total	1351629	3089266	70%
58	189	DISTRICT	Kushinagar	Total	1116973	2447571	69%
59	190	DISTRICT	Deoria	Total	876246	2224700	72%
60	191	DISTRICT	Azamgarh	Total	1372032	3241881	70%
61	192	DISTRICT	Mau	Total	696747	1509221	68%
62	193	DISTRICT	Ballia	Total	1019483	2220291	69%
63	194	DISTRICT	Jaunpur	Total	1437375	3056829	68%
64	195	DISTRICT	Ghazipur	Total	1204602	2415666	67%
65	196	DISTRICT	Chandauli	Total	652543	1300213	67%
66	197	DISTRICT	Varanasi	Total	1220708	2456133	67%
67	198	DISTRICT	SantRavidas Nagar (Bhadohi)	Total	470608	1107605	70%
68	199	DISTRICT	Mirzapur	Total	881996	1614974	65%
69	200	DISTRICT	Sonbhadra	Total	730399	1132160	61%
70	201	DISTRICT	Etah	Total	545984	1228496	69%
71	202	DISTRICT	Kanshiram Nagar	Total	472765	963954	67%

We can see from the above data that in each district, unemployment rate ranges from 60% - 70%. I couldn't believe it initially. I think some of the districts have been combined because the data had only 71 districts in it. The calculation I have done is by taking the number of population working and non-working. The aggregate of Uttar Pradesh comes out to be 67%.

Are these figures acceptable?

Don't you think the numbers should be the other way around?

It should be 67% of the population employed at least.

What needs to be done after data is collected i.e. arriving at the solution?

The 75 growing sectors which I think are the most promising for the current generation.

Sr. No.	Sector or Industry
1	Artificial Intelligence Industry
2	Gaming Industry
3	Power Instruments and Equipment Manufacturing Industry
4	Industrial and Commercial Machinery Industry
5	Stationery Industry
6	Virtual Reality and Visual Effects Industry
7	Software & Web Development Industry
8	Sports Goods & Equipment Industry
9	Hand & Power Tools Manufacturing Industry
10	Kitchen Tools & Machinery Manufacturing Industry
11	Animation Industry
12	Film Industry
13	Application Development Industry
14	Healthcare Industry
15	Building Equipment Industry
16	Chemical Industry
17	Carbon Fibre Manufacturing Industry

18	Mass Communications Industry
19	Metal Fabrication Industry
20	Bakery Goods Manufacturing Industry
21	Textile Industry
22	Packaged and Drinking Water Industry
23	Robotics Industry
24	Railway Industry
25	Defence Electronics Industry
26	Rubber and Miscellaneous Plastic Industry
27	Drones Manufacturing Industry
28	Hospitality Equipment Manufacturing Industry
29	Forex & Stock Market Research Industry
30	Ethical Hacking & Research Industry
31	Pharmaceutical Industry
32	Consumer Electronics Industry
33	Aviation Industry
34	Epoxy & Paint Manufacturing Industry
35	Pulp & Paper Manufacturing Industry
36	Food Processing Industry
37	Auto Components Industry
38	LED & Light Manufacturing Industry
39	Herbal & Ayurvedic Industry
40	Renewable Energy
41	Rubber and Plastics Footwear Industry
42	Music and Sound Industry
43	Leather Industry
44	Cosmetics Industry
45	Surgical Instruments Manufacturing Industry
46	Electronics Industry
47	Inland Water Transportation Industry
48	Arms & Ammunitions Industry
49	IT Industry
50	Fashion Industry

Continued...

51	Combat Vehicle Manufacturing Industry
52	Gem & Jewellery Manufacturing Industry
53	Education and Digital Education Industry
54	Apparel Industry
55	Bio-Manufacturing
56	Automobile Industry
57	Electrical Industry
58	Fabricated Metal Industry
59	Furniture and Fixtures Industry
60	Telecom Equipment Manufacturing Industry
61	Military Shipbuilding & Submarine Industry
62	Precast Concrete Manufacturing Industry
63	Agricultural Equipment Industry
64	Transportation Equipment Industry
65	Diamond Industry
66	Construction Equipment Industry
67	Stone, Clay, Glass, and Concrete Industry
68	Laser Instruments & Tools Manufacturing Industry
69	Language & Linguistic Learning Industry
70	Lumber and Wood Industry
71	Measuring, Analysing and Controlling Instrument Industry
72	Space Research
73	Scientific Equipment Manufacturing Industry
74	Defence Leather and Apparel Manufacturing Industry
75	Travel & Tourism Industry

"It is either you chase your dream or you run for survival"

1. Each district gets one specialised University in a particular sector.

2. Each district gets 5 major industries.

3. Each district gets 5 small scale industries.

4. Each district adopts one international sports or a sport which has a bright future in the upcoming years and maybe developing sports leagues.

5. Each district gets a proper and maintained sports center to promote a healthy lifestyle for its citizens.

6. Each District gets an institute under the government's Skill India where they would be taught on the topic of whichever industries are present in that district.

7. Each district gets proper and maintained healthcare which specialises in a particular disease or issue present in our bodies.

8. Each district on the basis of its cultural heritage gets to improve and promote itself as a tourist destination.

9. Depending on the cultural heritage development of museums for artifacts and art in the area.

10. Each district should get Entertainment centers.

11. Each district gets a helipad and a helicopter for situation like Disaster management, fire-fighting, rescue missions, medical emergencies and monitoring by the police. These can also be used as an institute to train professional helicopter pilots.

12. Uniting 5 Districts in the state, will get an airport i.e. that 5 districts will choose a center point for a new airport which will be connected to all the major cities in our country. This airport can be used to train pilots working as an institute. So, UP can have 15 new airports which will be connected with other states and countries and can also be used for air freight.

13. On the shore line of the major rivers or canals which are to be used as inland waterways in the future. Marine training institutes can also be established that particular district.

How to decide which industries are to be established out of 5 small scale and 5 major industries?

- The central government decides
  - 2 – major industries
  - 2 – Small scale industries
- The state government decides
  - 2 – major industries
  - 2 – small scale industries
- The district gets to decide
  - 1 – major industry
  - 1 – small scale industry

How will the districts decide?

By putting its promise fund i.e. District Promise Fund which each DM has, it could boost the development of the district.

What is District Promise Fund?

This fund is just the amount that each district is willing to put in that sector as a subsidy or for the establishment of an industry. This fund can be sourced from the fund which is under the administration of the District Magistrate.

When is it required?

During the decision-making process by the district in the selection of one small scale and major industry, where each district will bid for a particular industry and whoever bids the highest in a particular industry gets that industry in their district out of the 75 growing industries.

The entire selection process can be eased by the Vision Team and Business Development Department.

To understand how a district magistrate will decide and bid for a particular industry:

- We will collect all the data about the district

- Review the entire list of industries from which it could be chosen

- Take opinions from its citizens

- Let us say that the D. M. has 600 crore rupees in his fund

- After leaving all the emergency funds, healthcare funds, development funds and other funds, he is left with 120 crore rupees to spare

- This amount(120 crore rupees) becomes the District Promise fund

- Now the bidding of the industries happens for 1 major & 1 small scale industry

- Let us say that Aviation is the major industry and perfume being the small industry which the D.M along with the consideration of its citizens have mutually decided to bid for

- Let us say that the D.M. comes up with a number, 100 crore rupees, to be pledged under aviation and 20 crore rupees under perfume

- Now we are all aware of how bidding works. Whichever D.M. Bids the highest amount will get the industry in his district

- Now depending on the scale of the industry and the number of interested parties willing to invest in the district, this amount will be distributed as a subsidy to them in phases

- District cannot pledge on those industries which the central and state have already allotted..

Same is the case for selection by the central and state governments. How much are they willing to pledge as subsidy for that industry? As they have 2 of each to decide for every district, the central governments decide first from the list, then the state to decide and then the district. The state decides with help from the MP's (Member of Parliament) and MLA's (Member of Legislative Assembly) of those regions. They can also pledge their funds as Promise funds to help establish more and more industries in their region.

Example for Sector or Industry in each District

Sr. No.	District		Sectors or Industries
1	Agra	→	Artificial Intelligence Industry
2	Aligarh	→	Gaming Industry
3	Ambedkar Nagar	→	Power Instruments and Equipment Manufacturing Industry
4	Amethi (ChatrapatiSahujiMahraj Nagar)	→	Industrial and Commercial Machinery Industry
5	Amroha (J.P. Nagar)	→	Stationery Industry
6	Auraiya	→	Virtual Reality and Visual Effects Industry
7	Ayodhya	→	Software & Web Development Industry
8	Azamgarh	→	Sports Goods & Equipment Industry
9	Baghpat	→	Hand & Power Tools Manufacturing Industry
10	Bahraich	→	Kitchen Tools &Machinery Manufacturing Industry
11	Ballia	→	Animation Industry
12	Balrampur	→	Film Industry
13	Banda	→	Application Development Industry
14	Barabanki	→	Healthcare Industry

15	Bareilly	→	Building Equipment Industry
16	Basti	→	Chemical Industry
17	Bhadohi	→	Carbon Fibre Manufacturing Industry
18	Bijnor	→	Mass Communications Industry
19	Budaun	→	Metal Fabrication Industry
20	Bulandshahr	→	Bakery Goods Manufacturing Industry
21	Chandauli	→	Textile Industry
22	Chitrakoot	→	Packaged and Drinking Water Industry
23	Deoria	→	Robotics Industry
24	Etah	→	Railway Industry
25	Etawah	→	Defence Electronics Industry
26	Farrukhabad	→	Rubber and Miscellaneous Plastic Industry
27	Fatehpur	→	Drones Manufacturing Industry
28	Firozabad	→	Hospitality Equipment Manufacturing Industry
29	Gautam Buddha Nagar	→	Forex & Stock Market Research Industry
30	Ghaziabad	→	Ethical Hacking & Research Industry
31	Ghazipur	→	Pharmaceutical Industry
32	Gonda	→	Consumer Electronics Industry
33	Gorakhpur	→	Aviation Industry
34	Hamirpur	→	Epoxy & Paint Manufacturing Industry
35	Hapur (Panchsheel Nagar)	→	Pulp & Paper Manufacturing Industry
36	Hardoi	→	Food Processing Industry
37	Hathras	→	Auto Components Industry
38	Jalaun	→	LED & Light Manufacturing Industry

Continued...

39	Jaunpur	→	Herbal & Ayurvedic Industry
40	Jhansi	→	Renewable Energy
41	Kannauj	→	Rubber and Plastics Footwear Industry
42	Kanpur Dehat	→	Music and Sound Industry
43	Kanpur Nagar	→	Leather Industry
44	Kanshiram Nagar (Kasganj)	→	Cosmetics Industry
45	Kaushambi	→	Surgical Instruments Manufacturing Industry
46	Kushinagar (Padrauna)	→	Electronics Industry
47	Lakhimpur – Kheri	→	Inland Water Transportation Industry
48	Lalitpur	→	Arms & Ammunitions Industry
49	Lucknow	→	IT Industry
50	Maharajganj	→	Fashion Industry
51	Mahoba	→	Combat Vehicle Manufacturing Industry
52	Mainpuri	→	Gem & Jewellery Manufacturing Industry
53	Mathura	→	Education and Digital Education Industry
54	Mau	→	Apparel Industry
55	Meerut	→	Bio-Manufacturing Industry
56	Mirzapur	→	Automobile Industry
57	Moradabad	→	Electrical Industry
58	Muzaffarnagar	→	Fabricated Metal Industry
59	Pilibhit	→	Furniture and Fixtures Industry
60	Pratapgarh	→	Telecom Equipment Manufacturing Industry
61	Prayagraj	→	Military Shipbuilding & Submarine Industry
62	Raebareli	→	Precast Concrete Manufacturing Industry
63	Rampur	→	Agricultural Equipment Industry

64	Saharanpur	→	Transportation Equipment Industry
65	Sambhal (Bhim Nagar)	→	Diamond Industry
66	Sant Kabir Nagar	→	Construction Equipment Industry
67	Shahjahanpur	→	Stone, Clay, Glass, and Concrete Industry
68	Shamali (Prabuddh Nagar)	→	Laser Instruments & Tools Manufacturing Industry
69	Shravasti	→	Language & Linguistic Learning Industry
70	Siddharth Nagar	→	Lumber and Wood Industry
71	Sitapur	→	Measuring, Analysing and Controlling Instrument Industry
72	Sonbhadra	→	Space Research
73	Sultanpur	→	Scientific Equipment Manufacturing Industry
74	Unnao	→	Defence Leather and Apparel Manufacturing Industry
75	Varanasi	→	Travel & Tourism Industry

The above is just an example to show you how it can be achieved by allotting one industry to each district. But actually, a district will get at least 5 of each major and small scale industries to start with to get more and more investments coming in our state. There are various other industries apart from the ones mentioned above which the government can think of to be allotted to a district.

Other industries can also be setup in that region but the major subsidy will be given to those industries which have been selected. Call it subsidy or Business Establishment Funds but they both mean the same thing.

How to decide the specialised University for each district?

This can be achieved mutually by the District, State, Central, demands from the district, the Education department, the Vision Team and

Business Development Department. The Promise Fund from the district can be used to develop these Universities.

Below data is a just representation of what governments can develop in terms of a University in each district so that specialised education in different sectors can be provided.

Example for a University In each District

Sr. No.	District		Universities
1	Agra	→	Electrical University
2	Aligarh	→	Scientific Equipment Research & Development University
3	Ambedkar Nagar	→	Gaming University
4	Amethi (ChatrapatiSahujiMahraj Nagar)	→	Defence Electronics University
5	Amroha (J.P. Nagar)	→	Application Development University
6	Auraiya	→	Bio-Research & Development University
7	Ayodhya	→	Ancient Research & Technology University
8	Azamgarh	→	Telecom Equipment Research & Development University
9	Baghpat	→	Military Shipbuilding & Submarine University
10	Bahraich	→	LED & Light Research & Development University
11	Ballia	→	Apparel Research& Development University
12	Balrampur	→	Stationery Research & Development University
13	Banda	→	Hospitality Research & Development University

14	Barabanki	→	Consumer Electronics University
15	Bareilly	→	Forex & Stock Market Research University
16	Basti	→	Robotics Research & Development University
17	Bhadohi	→	Diamond Processing and Research University
18	Bijnor	→	Education and Digital Education University
19	Budaun	→	Artificial Intelligence University
20	Bulandshahr	→	IT University
21	Chandauli	→	Architectural University
22	Chitrakoot	→	Mass Communications University
23	Deoria	→	Renewable Energy
24	Etah	→	Surgical Instruments Research & Development University
25	Etawah	→	Metal Fabrication University
26	Farrukhabad	→	Sports Goods & Equipment University
27	Fatehpur	→	Transportation Equipment University
28	Firozabad	→	Combat Vehicle Research & Development University
29	Gautam Buddha Nagar	→	Fabricated Metal University
30	Ghaziabad	→	Kitchen Tools & Machinery Research & Development University
31	Ghazipur	→	Rubber and Plastics Footwear University
32	Gonda	→	Ethical Hacking & Research University
33	Gorakhpur	→	Chemical University
34	Hamirpur	→	Language & Linguistic Studies University

Continued...

35	Hapur (Panchsheel Nagar)	→	Bakery Goods Research & Development University
36	Hardoi	→	Power Instruments and Equipment Research & Development University
37	Hathras	→	Measuring, Analysing and Controlling Instrument University
38	Jalaun	→	Industrial and Commercial Machinery University
39	Jaunpur	→	Precast Concrete Research & Development University
40	Jhansi	→	Travel &Tourism University
41	Kannauj	→	Epoxy & Paint Research & Development University
42	Kanpur Dehat	→	Space Research & Development University
43	Kanpur Nagar	→	Software & Web Development University
44	Kanshiram Nagar (Kasganj)	→	Mineral Research University
45	Kaushambi	→	Virtual Reality and Visual Effects University
46	Kushinagar (Padrauna)	→	Defence Leather and Apparel Research & Development University
47	Lakhimpur - Kheri	→	Electronics University
48	Lalitpur	→	Civil Construction and Structure University
49	Lucknow	→	Auto Components University
50	Maharajganj	→	Film University
51	Mahoba	→	Agricultural Equipment Research University
52	Mainpuri	→	Cosmetics University
53	Mathura	→	Automobile University

54	Mau	→	Laser Instruments & Tools Research & Development University
55	Meerut	→	Railway University
56	Mirzapur	→	Fashion University
57	Moradabad	→	Inland Water Transportation University
58	Muzaffarnagar	→	Furniture and Fixtures University
59	Pilibhit	→	Healthcare University
60	Pratapgarh	→	Arms & Ammunitions Research & Development University
61	Prayagraj	→	Textile University
62	Raebareli	→	Music and Sound University
63	Rampur	→	Rubber and Miscellaneous Plastic University
64	Saharanpur	→	Hand & Power Tools Research & Development University
65	Sambhal (Bhim Nagar)	→	Food Processing University
66	Sant Kabir Nagar	→	Leather University
67	Shahjahanpur	→	Drones Research & Development University
68	Shamali (Prabuddh Nagar)	→	Animation Research & Development University
69	Shravasti	→	Aviation University
70	Siddharth Nagar	→	Carbon Fibre Research & Development University
71	Sitapur	→	Pharmaceutical University
72	Sonbhadra	→	Packaged and Drinking Water University
73	Sultanpur	→	Pulp & Paper Research & Development University
74	Unnao	→	Gem & Jewellery Research & Development University
75	Varanasi	→	Herbal & Ayurvedic Research & Development University

How do you perceive this idea?

Can we achieve more in each sector if we distribute them and study them descriptively?

In this process each University gets a mentor. What I mean is that the leading experts in that sector can take that particular university under their supervision and monitor them. Like what the courses are or improving the course structures, the kind of practical courses that are needed and how will they be useful in the industry. This could be a part of their CSR (Corporate Social Responsibility) which helps in getting them their tax benefits.

Note: Just to ensure that any one particular district does not have market dominance in a particular sector or industry, no district will have the same course offered in the University as that of the industry present in that district. This is so that the cash flow is maintained.

Infrastructure requirements can be reduced by introducing e-learning for certain parts present in the course.

Chapter 20

Research & Development

Research and development basically means that finding the best possible solution for a problem or a problem that might arise in the future. It could be the industrial demands, technological demands, healthcare demands, defense demands or any other demand which is required by the current or the future generations.

"Make, create and innovate"

Why is it important?

For the growth of any country the development of R&D in various sectors is very crucial. The requirements are constantly changing and the trends are changing to keep up with the requirements of the current generation R&D facilities which are a must.

"The world is changing if we don't adapt fast; we are going to lose it all."

Strategy to implement this into a state is by:

Initially selecting 7 sectors and 7 districts to establish and run these facilities which have the most amount of District Promise Fund.

Examples

Sr. No.	District		Research & Development
1	Agra	→	Artificial Intelligence & Supercomputing Research & Development Centre
2	Bareilly	→	Construction Research & Development Centre
3	Gorakhpur	→	Transportation Research & Development Centre
4	Lucknow	→	Bio-Medical Research & Development Centre
5	Prayagraj	→	Defence Research & Development Centre
6	Sonbhadra	→	Space Research & Development Centre
7	Varanasi	→	Chemical Research & Development Centre

In smaller sectors this can be done in Universities itself but in certain sectors, data breach or leaking of data could become a major issue and hence the need for dedicated facilities is very crucial. And we cannot privatise this also as certain research should be led by the government.

"Innovation is the key to success"

Seven sectors that the government should really focus on are:

1. Artificial Intelligence and Supercomputing Research & Development Centre

2. Construction Research & Development Centre

3. Transportation Research & Development Centre

4. Bio-Medical Research & Development Centre

5. Defense Research & Development Centre

6. Space Research & Development Centre

7. Chemical Research & Development Centre

These fields require more expertise and hence there is more requirement of improvement so that India becomes a market leader in the sector of research. From being a developing country, India becomes a developed country.

Chapter 21

Supercomputers & Data Servers

We are living in the age of supercomputing where all the data needs to be processed efficiently and at a fast rate. As the world and our country is moving towards a digital age, the need for more Supercomputers and Data server is increasing as well.

Each state must have a Supercomputer of its own so that the working of each state becomes easier. In the world of AI, this becomes an obligation.

Why are Data servers necessary?

A shift towards cloud computing is very important for the data flowing in the state, the country and outside the country remains safe and secure. Government data should not be accessible to unauthorised parties and a data breach could be very harmful for a country.

In a state like ours which is comparable to many countries, at least 2 Supercomputers are a must and at least 10 Data Servers so that monitoring and managing becomes easy.

Example

Supercomputers

Sr. No.	District		Supercomputers
1	Gautam Buddha Nagar	→	GautumBuddh Supercomputer
4	Jaunpur	→	Atala Devi Supercomputer

Data Servers

Sr. No.	District		Data Servers
1	Bahraich	→	Saryu Data Server Centre
2	Bijnor	→	Sita Maa Data Server Centre
3	Ghazipur	→	Maharishi Jamadagini Data Server Centre
4	Lalitpur	→	Neelkantheshwar Data Server Centre
5	Maharajganj	→	Adaruna Devi Data Server Centre
6	Mainpuri	→	Saman Data Server Centre
7	Mathura	→	Bhagwan Krishna Data Server Centre
8	Pratapgarh	→	Raja PratapBhadur Singh Data Server Centre
9	Shahjahanpur	→	Ram Prasad Bismil Data Server Centre
10	Sonbhadra	→	Kashi Data Server Centre

The above example is just to give you an idea.

These targets can be easily achieved by the Vision Team by its Vision Fund. We are seeing a digital future where most of us will be busy in our routines connected by these future interfaces. Collecting and storing data is also very important so that it can be easily available to anyone and everyone for certain parts and available for our future generations to come.

Glossary

1. **Aadamee or aadmiyon: - Person or people**

2. **Aadhar: - Unique Identity Card in India**

3. **Aaen: - Come**

4. **Aam: - Common**

5. **Aap: - You**

6. **Aarahi: - Coming**

7. **Aarthik: - Economic**

8. **Aaye: - Come**

9. **Ab: - Now**

10. **Acha: - Good**

11. **Aega: - Coming**

12. **Agale: - Next**

13. **Agar: - If**

14. **Aisee: - Such**

15. **Alag: - Different**

16. **Apani: - Mine**

17. **Apne: - Ours**

18. **Aree: - Hey**

19. **Aur: - And or further**

20. **B. Com: - Bachelors of Commerce**

21. **B. Sc: - Bachelors of science**

22. **B. Tech: - Bachelors of Technology**

23. **Baakee: - Rest**

24. **Baar: - Times**

25. **Baat: - Talk**

26. **Baatein: - Coversation**

27. **Bach: - Escape**

28. **Bachane: - Escaping**

29. **Badalana or Badalane: - To Change**

30. **Badee or bade: - Big**

31. **Badha: - Increase**

32. **Badhaana: - Increasing**

33. **Bahut: - Very**

34. **Bajane: - Ringing**

35. **Bana or Banate: - Create**

36. **Bas: - Enough**

37. **Bataenge: - Will tell**

38. **Batao: - Tell**

39. **Bataya: - Told**

40. **BBA: - Bachelors in Business Administration**

41. **Bechaare: - Poor or pitiful**

42. **Bewakoofon: - Stupid**

43. **Bhagwan: - God**

44. **Bharee or Bharte: - Full off**

45. **Bhi: - Too**

46. **Bilkul: - Absolutely**

47. **Boldo or Bolo: - Speak**

48. **Bulaatee: - Calling**

49. **Chaatane: - Licking**

50. **Chahiye: - Ought to have**

51. **Chalata: - To operate**

52. **Chali: - Gone**

53. **Cheej: - Thing**

54. **Cheejein or Cheejon: - Things**

55. **Chhod: - Leave**

56. **Chidiya: - Bird**

57. **Chinta: - Worry**

58. **Chotee: - Small**

59. **Chunautiyon: - Difficulties**

60. **Chupate: - Hiding**

61. **Chutkee: - Snapping of Fingers**

62. **CM: - Chief Minister**

63. **CSR: - Corporate Social Responsbility**

64. **Dard: - Pain**

65. **Dekhayega: - Will See**

66. **Dekhiye: - Look at it**

67. **Dekhna: - To See**

68. **Dena: - To be Given**

69. **Denge: - Will**

70. **Desh: - Country**

71. **Dete: - Give**

72. **Dhyaan: - Care**

73. **Di: - Given**

74. **Dijiyega or dijiye: - To Give**

75. **Din: - Day**

76. **DM: - District Magistrate**

77. **Dookaan: - Shop**

78. **Doosare: - Secondly or Others**

79. **DPF: - District Promise Fund**

80. **Duniya: - World**

81. **Ek: - One**

82. **Faayada or Faayade: - Benifit**

83. **Farak: - Affect**

84. **FDI: - Foreign direct Investment**

85. **Galatee: - Mistake**

86. **Galatiyon: - Mistakes**

87. **Gaya: - Gone**

88. **GMS: - Government Management Service**

89. **Goonjega: - Echo**

90.   **GS: -Government Switch**

91.   **GST: - Goods & Services Tax**

92.   **Haath: - Hand**

93.   **Hafte: - Week**

94.   **Hai: - Is**

95.   **Hain: - Huh**

96.   **Hamaare: - Our**

97.   **Hame: - Us**

98.   **Har: - Every**

99.   **Hindustan: - Indian or India**

100.   **Hisab: - Account**

101.   **Ho: - Be or Happen**

102.   **Hoga: - Will be done**

103.   **Hogaya: - Has been done**

104.   **Hojayega: - Will be Done**

105.   **Hona: - Turn out**

106.   **Hota or Hote: - Happen**

107.   **Hua: - Happened**

108.   **Hum: - We**

109.   **Humaara or Humaare: - Our**

110.   **Hume: - We Should**

111.   **Humne: - We are**

112.   **IGRS: - Integrated Grievances Redress System**

113.   **IIM: - Indian Institute of Mangement**

114. **IIT: - Indian Institute of Technology**

115. **Inaka: - Their**

116. **Insaan: - Human**

117. **Isko: - This**

118. **Iss: - Is**

119. **IT: - Information Technology**

120. **Itne: - So**

121. **Jaatee: - Go**

122. **Jaaye: - Will go**

123. **Jaayega: - Will be going**

124. **Jahaan: - Where**

125. **Janaab: - Sir**

126. **Janam: - Birthplace**

127. **Jang: - War**

128. **Jara: - A bit of**

129. **Jiski: - Whose**

130. **Jo: - What**

131. **Jyaada: - More**

132. **Kaam: - Work**

133. **Kab: - When**

134. **Kahan: - Where**

135. **Kaise: - How**

136. **Kal: - Tomorrow**

137. **Kalam: - Pen**

138. **Kamaoge: - Earn**

139. **Kami or Kamiyon: - Short Comings**

140. **Kanun: - Law**

141. **Kar: - Do it**

142. **Karavana or karna: - Doing**

143. **Karo: - To Do**

144. **Karttavy: - Duty**

145. **Karva: - Get it Done**

146. **Ke: - The**

147. **Keh or Kehne: - Speak**

148. **Khaasa: - Quite**

149. **Kharche: - Expenses**

150. **Khol: - Open**

151. **Kisakee: - Whose**

152. **Kitne: - How many**

153. **Kon: - Who**

154. **Konasee: - Which one**

155. **Krpa: - Mercy**

156. **Kuch: - Something**

157. **Kya: - What**

158. **Lad: - Fight**

159. **Ladenge: - Fighting**

160. **Laga: - Give**

161. **Lagavana: - Giving**

162. **Lagegee: - To Be Given**

163. **Layen or Lene: - To Bring**

164. **Leejiyega: - Take**

165. **Leke: - To Bring**

166. **Lo: - Give**

167. **Log or Logon: - People**

168. **M. Tech: - Masters in Technology**

169. **M.Com: - Masters in Commerce**

170. **M.Sc: - Masters of Science**

171. **Maahir: - Expert**

172. **Maanasik: - Mentally Health**

173. **Maanga: - To Take**

174. **Maarta: - To Push**

175. **Madam: - Maam**

176. **Maheene: - Month**

177. **Majbooree: - Helplessness**

178. **Mana: - Refuse**

179. **Mantri or Mantriji: - Minister**

180. **Mantriyon: - Ministers**

181. **MBA: - Masters In Business Administration**

182. **Mehanat: - Hard work**

183. **Mein: - Into**

184. **Milao: - To Meet**

185. **MLA: - Member of Legislative Assembly**

186. **MP: - Member of Parliament**

187. **Muh: - Mouth**

188. **Mulaakaat: - Meeting**

189. **Mushkil: - Difficulty**

190. **Naam: - Name**

191. **Naaraaz: - Angry**

192. **Nahi: - No**

193. **Naukaree: - Job**

194. **Netas: - Politicians**

195. **NIC: - National Informatics Center**

196. **Nikal: - Gone**

197. **Nikalvaane: - Remove**

198. **Niyam: - Rules**

199. **Paas: - Near**

200. **Padega: - Will Have to**

201. **Pahunch: - To reach**

202. **Paisa: - Money**

203. **Par: - But**

204. **Pareshaan: - Anxious or Stressed**

205. **Pasand: - To Like Something**

206. **Pata: - Know**

207. **Patthar: - Rock**

208. **Pichhali or Pichhale: - Last Time**

209. **Poore: - Whole**

210. **Pradesh:** - State

211. **Prati:** - Per

212. **Puri:** - Complete

213. **PWD:** - Public Works Department

214. **R & D:** - Reseach and Development

215. **Raha:** - There Is

216. **Rahe:** - There are

217. **Rahenge:** - There will be

218. **Rakh:** - Keep

219. **Rakhegi:** - Keeping

220. **Rattu:** - Mugging up word to word

221. **Roj:** - Daily

222. **Rupiya:** - Rupees

223. **Saal:** - Year

224. **Sab:** - Whole

225. **Sabajiwala:** - Vegetable Seller

226. **Sahab:** - Sir

227. **Sahi:** - Good

228. **Sake or Sakta:** - Could

229. **Samajho:** - Understand

230. **Samay:** - Time

231. **Sari:** - Whole

232. **Sarkar:** - Goverment

233. **Se:** - From

234. **Seene: - Chest**

235. **Sirf: - Only**

236. **Sochata: - Thinks**

237. **Sone: - Gold**

238. **SSSE: - State Startup Stock Exchange**

239. **Sthiti: - Situation**

240. **Sunanee: - To Tell**

241. **Tak or Taki: - Till**

242. **Tankha: - Salary**

243. **Tarah: - Kind**

244. **Tehsil: - Township**

245. **Tha or Thi: - Was**

246. **Thela or Thelawala: - Trolley for selling Goods or food**

247. **Thoda or Thodee: - Little**

248. **Toh: - Then**

249. **Tota: - Parrot**

250. **Tum or Tumhe: - You and Yours**

251. **Udyog Aadhar: - Unique Identification Number for Businesses in India**

252. **Unake: - Their**

253. **UP: - Uttar Pradesh**

254. **UPSC: - Union Public Service Commisson**

255. **Usaka: - Its or His**

256. **Usakee: - Their**

257. **Uss: - That**

258. **Vajah: - Reason**

259. **Valon: - Related to**

260. **Vishay: - Subject**

261. **Vo or Woh: - That**

262. **Wala: - The one**

263. **Wese: - Else**

264. **Yaad: - Remember**

265. **Yahin: - Right Here**

266. **Ye or Yeh: - These**

267. **Yojana: - Policies**

268. **Zaroorat or Zarooree: - Important**

269. **Zarooraton Necessary**

270. **Zindagi: - Life**